The most en
pleasure to re
amazing clari
an entertainir
wonderful help for the sceptic, the seeker, and the believer. I hope
that the authors have an eye to writing further volumes on equally
essential topics of the Christian faith. They are most needed!

Paul David Washer
President, Heart Cry Ministry, Radford, Virginia

Thirty years ago I sat in my bibliology class in seminary,
desperately trying to understand the truths that my professor was
trying to convey. It was a very edifying class, and the content I
grasped helped to equip me for three decades of ministry. I am
sincerely thankful for those lectures. However, I wish that this
book had been available to me in 1989. It is so refreshing to
read such a practical book with such vivid illustrations on such a
complex topic. This should be mandatory reading for all seminary
students! What also heightens my enjoyment of the book is my
personal friendship with Andrew Mathieson. It's my hope that
this will become an audio book and that the author himself will
have the responsibility of reading it. It would be akin to 'Shrek
meets Carl F. H. Henry!'

Ed Moore
Head Pastor, North Shore Baptist Church, Bayside, New York

Christian Focus Publications, 20Schemes and 9Marks are to be
congratulated on their collaboration on the First Steps series, as
they take seriously the challenge of preparing materials designed
to equip those from an unchurched background as they begin
their Christian life.

In keeping with this mission, the text of this book on the Bible
is helpfully broken up into readily-digestible, bite-size pieces
which pose questions, provide small chunks of teaching and

also relevant illustrations and scenarios from the life of Reenie, a new Christian from an unchurched background, and her as yet unbelieving husband, Pete. The layout of almost every page is slightly different and that, with the variety of fonts and line-spacings, helps the readability of the book.

The volume covers topics such as the origins of the Bible, its trustworthiness, its relevance for today, some of its major themes and the fact that it all points to Jesus. While helping young Christians from unchurched backgrounds to understand some of the great teachings of the Bible, the book also introduces them to some of the great biblical and theological terms such as special revelation, inspiration, Messiah, kingdom, covenant and substitution, no doubt preparing them for further study and growth in their understanding of their new-found faith.

Hector Morrison
Principal, Highland Theological College, Dingwall

I've spent the last 12 years in pastoral ministry trying to get people to know their Bibles. Lately, I've realized that knowing the Bible doesn't matter unless they trust it. I wish I had this helpful resource when I was starting 12 years ago. It's short and sweet. Profoundly simple, incredibly insightful, and comprehensively concise. I can't think of a better starting point for anyone beginning their Christian journey (or refreshing the foundations) than this resource on trusting the Bible! I look forward to using this book for years to come.

John Onwuchekwa
Lead Pastor, Cornerstone Church, Atlanta, Georgia

IX 9Marks | First Steps Series

BIBLE

CAN WE TRUST IT?

ANDREW MATHIESON
SERIES EDITED BY MEZ MCCONNELL

CHRISTIAN
FOCUS

IX 9Marks

Copyright © Andrew Mathieson 2019

paperback ISBN 978-1-5271-0000-8
epub ISBN 978-1-5271-0343-6
mobi ISBN 978-1-5271-0344-3

10 9 8 7 6 5 4 3 2 1

Published in 2019
by
Christian Focus Publications Ltd,
Geanies House, Fearn, Ross-shire,
IV20 1TW, Great Britain.
www.christianfocus.com

Cover and interior
design by Rubner Durais

Printed and bound
by Bell & Bain, Glasgow

CONTENTS

PREFACE

Hi there I'm Andrew Mathieson, Husband to Lauren, father of Talia and Stephen with another little girl due in June 2019.

Today I'm the lead pastor and planter of Lochee Baptist Chapel, in Dundee, Scotland. But a little over twelve years ago I was your stereotypical guitar playing scheme pothead complete with Noel Gallagheresque delusions of grandeur.

I had the privilege of growing up in a Christian home, in a nice part of town. I was familiar with the gospel and the Scriptures from my youth, but back then I wanted nothing to do them. Through my own sin and mess at seventeen I ended up homeless and eventually landed up 'living the dream' in a little scheme called Hillhead in Glasgow, Scotland. (Scheme is a Scottish term for the socially disadvantaged housing estates that are home to over a quarter of Scotland's population.)

During the years that I lived there my mother faithfully continued to share the gospel with me and call me to repentance and faith in Christ, but in the scheme I only ever heard the name Jesus used as curse word and never came into contact with a Bible – neither did anyone else, which is a tragedy.

In 2 Timothy 3:15 we learn that the Scriptures, are able to give us wisdom for salvation through faith in Jesus.

Let me put it plainly, where the Scripture aren't heard there is only a hopeless certainty of hell.

By God's grace alone I heard the Scriptures, encountered Jesus and was saved. He turned my life upside down gave me love of His Word and has taken me from pothead to pastor.

This book exists to explain what the Bible is, where it came from, and what it's about, in simple terms that the guys I used to kick about with could understand.

It's dedicated to my mum, Ruth. Thank-you for loving me, telling me about Jesus and for teaching me to, 'Trust in the LORD with all my heart, and not lean on my own understanding.'

It is my hope and prayer that the Lord will use this book to give others a life transforming love of Jesus and His Word.

Soli Deo Gloria.

ANDREW MATHIESON
Lochee, Dundee.

SERIES INTRODUCTION

The First Steps series will help equip those from an unchurched background take the first steps in following Jesus. We call this the 'pathway to service' as we believe that every Christian should be equipped to be of service to Christ and His church no matter your background or life experience.

If you are a church leader doing ministry in hard places, use these books as a tool to help grow those who are unfamiliar with the teachings of Jesus into new disciples. These books will equip them to grow in character, knowledge and action.

Or if you yourself are new to the Christian faith, still struggling to make sense of what a Christian is, or what the Bible actually says, then this is an easy to understand guide as you take your first steps as a follower of Jesus.

There are many ways to use these books.

+ They could be used by an individual who simply reads through the content and works through the questions on their own.

+ They could be used in a one-to-one setting, where two people read through the material before they meet and then discuss the questions together.

+ They could be used in a group setting where a leader presents the material as a talk, stopping for group discussion throughout.

Your setting will determine how you best use this resource.

A USER'S KEY:

As you work through the studies you will come across the following symbols…

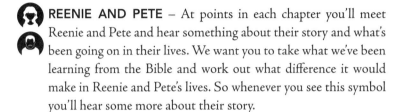 **REENIE AND PETE** – At points in each chapter you'll meet Reenie and Pete and hear something about their story and what's been going on in their lives. We want you to take what we've been learning from the Bible and work out what difference it would make in Reenie and Pete's lives. So whenever you see this symbol you'll hear some more about their story.

ILLUSTRATION – Through real-life examples and scenarios, these sections help us to understand the point that's being made.

STOP – When we hit an important or hard point we'll ask you to stop and spend some time thinking or chatting through what we've just learnt. This might be answering some questions, or it might be hearing more of Reenie and Pete's story.

KEY VERSE – The Bible is God's Word to us, and therefore it is the final word to us on everything we are to believe and how we are to behave. Therefore we want to read the Bible first, and we want to read it carefully. So whenever you see this symbol you are to read or listen to the Bible passage three times. If the person you're reading the Bible with feels comfortable, get them to read it at least once.

MEMORY VERSE – At the end of each chapter we'll suggest a Bible verse for memorisation. We have found Bible memorisation to be really effective in our context. The verse (or verses) will be directly related to what we've covered in the chapter.

SUMMARY – Also, at the end of each chapter we've included a short summary of the content of that chapter. If you're working your way through the book with another person, this might be useful to revisit when picking up from a previous week.

MEET REENIE AND PETE

We met Reenie a few years ago when she came to our Christmas Service. *'It's what you do at Christmas after all.'* Reenie is a wee gem, salt of the earth. She genuinely would do anything for anyone. She's been married to Pete for years. They have four kids who are all grown up and they have seven grandkids. We see her grandkids a lot at our church youth clubs and Reenie looks after them most days after school and all through the school holidays. The last few months she has really struggled with the older boys now that they have reached their teenage years. The boys have always been cheeky but recently one of them crossed the line, swearing and pushing his nan. It was so bad Pete had to step in and sort it out. *'Pete was so mad,'* Reenie tells us, *'I thought he was going to beat them there and then.'*

One morning Reenie suffered a health scare and ended up in the Accident & Emergency room. She suffered a mini heart attack and it's caused her to re-evaluate her life. She has begun to think about dying for the first time in her life. She has even been to the funeral directors to get a payment plan sorted to pay for her funeral.

Reenie would consider herself a spiritual person. In fact, she comes from a Catholic family. She went through her first communion as a young girl and married Pete in the local Catholic church. She describes herself as, 'A holiday Christian,' meaning she only really attends at Christmas and Easter.

We don't really see too much of Pete at the church. In fact, at times he appears to be a bit hostile towards Christians. He definitely isn't shy in sharing his opinion! After much prayer and perseverance, Pete eventually began attending services with Reenie, and eventually both came to faith in Jesus.

INTRODUCTION

'Fairytales!'; 'Made up stories for weirdos'; 'a bigoted rulebook'; 'irrelevant and out of date'; 'inaccurate and incomprehensible'; 'a self-help manual'; 'a mad history book'; 'dead interesting'; 'God's Word'.

These are a few of the responses I've heard and received when talking to lads and lassies in Lochee about the Bible. Their opinions are really interesting because none of them have ever actually read one.

Why would they?

It is far easier to believe the world around us and what they think about the Christian faith and the Bible. Add the influence of the Roman Catholic Church and the liberal national church into the mix and we have a recipe for confusion. How can people have confidence in the Bible when:

They're taught that the church places itself above the Bible as the ultimate authority.

> **The local Priest or Minister doesn't have confidence and trust in the Bible.**

> > **National church leaders seem to make the Bible mean whatever they want it to mean in order to try and fit in with modern culture.**

All this confusion means that people in the schemes have a few questions when it comes to the Word of God.

Can we really trust it?

Where does it come from?

How was it put together?

Who decided what to put in and what to leave out?

What do we mean when we say it's inspired?

Is it really 100% true?

What's this Old and New Testament jargon?

Hasn't science basically disproved the Bible?

'What do you mean it's all about Jesus? That just doesn't make sense,' Reenie would say. Even though she would say that she's a Christian she still struggles with the point of the Bible. '*I know some of it. There's the Ten Commandments. I suppose we need to try and obey them. But what good is the rest of it to my life?*'

Reenie's not the only one that struggles with questions like these. This book exists to answer her questions so that people in schemes, estates, projects, townships and trailer-parks **can be completely confident in the Bible**

They can trust 100% in the gospel it reveals to us.

Through the Bible they can come to know, love and serve King Jesus.

The book of 2 Timothy was written, from a prison cell, by the Apostle Paul. He would soon be put to death for his faith and so he writes to one of his young apprentices, Timothy, in order to help him pastor a church in a town called Ephesus. This place was messed up. People were spiritually confused. There were new

Christians, like Reenie & Pete, who knew next to nothing about the Bible. So, Paul reminds this young pastor about what the Bible is, what it does and how it does it.

'But as for you, continue in what you have learned and firmly believed. You know those who taught you, and you know that from infancy you have known the sacred Scriptures, which are able to give you wisdom for salvation through faith in Christ Jesus. All Scripture is inspired by God and is profitable for teaching, for rebuking, for correcting, for training in righteousness, so that the man of God may be complete, equipped for every good work' (2 Tim. 3:14-17).

The Bible is God's Word.

Paul tells us in these verses that the Bible is able to make us

wise for salvation,

through faith in Jesus Christ.

All of the Bible has been inspired by God.

Paul tells us that **all of it is profitable** for us because:

It teaches us.

It rebukes us.

It corrects us.

It trains us in righteousness.

That means **the Bible is very important in the life of a Christian.** *So much so that Paul tells us:*

'Through it we may become complete,
Equipped for every good work' (2 Tim. 3:17).

WHAT'S THE POINT?

GOD wrote the Bible to save sinners.

1. WHERE DID THE BIBLE COME FROM?
PART I (ORIGINS)

STOP

Where do you think the Bible comes from?

You probably have a lot of questions about the Bible, and if you are going to believe and trust what it says, these questions need answers. But, before we get to where the Bible comes from, we need to ask,

'Why does the Bible exist?'

We ended our intro by saying that the Bible is God's Word, able to make us wise for salvation, through faith in Jesus Christ. In turn, it then makes us useful to Jesus as we live out our lives. Let's spend some time thinking this through.

Firstly, **all of the Bible is God's Word**. The first proper line of the Bible introduces us to the main character, hero and author of the book.

'In the beginning God created the heavens and the earth' (Gen. 1:1).

This verse gives us some seriously important information. **God is** the **creator**, **ruler** and **owner** of *everything*. If we continue to read that first chapter of the Bible then we'll notice something else about God.

STOP

Look at Genesis chapter one. What two words do we see at the beginning of nearly every verse? (Heads up: When something is repeated in the Bible then it means it's important.)

God speaks. In fact, the phrase 'God said' shows up 10 times in the first chapter of Genesis.

God is a communicator.

He creates the universe and everything in it by speaking.

This is important for us to understand because it is God's nature as a communicator and His desire to communicate with us, as the pinnacle of His creation, that explains the ultimate origins of the Bible.

 ILLUSTRATION

When Pete was a child, his dad worked in a shipyard on the River Clyde and every so often he would take him to watch the launch of a new battleship out of the dry dock into the river. As a small boy he remembered being amazed by these massive frigates and wondering how they came to be. What did it take to design one? How were they built? He'd pester his dad with these questions all morning. Even as a child, Pete knew that a marvel of engineering like a Royal Navy frigate didn't simply appear out of thin air. Someone designed it and built it and, in the case of a frigate, many people were involved in the process. Just by looking at the ship, Pete could learn lots of things about these mysterious builders. He knew they were creative, intelligent and skillful.

The same is true of the universe that God created. It gives us lots of information about God. Its size and detail tells us that **God is massive, intelligent, powerful, wise,** and **skillful.** The beauty and diversity of the universe tells us that **God is creative**, **artistic**, **beautiful** and **glorious**.

 'The heavens declare the glory of God, and the expanse proclaims the work of his hands. Day after day they pour out speech; night after night they communicate knowledge' (Ps. 19:1-2).

The universe just won't shut up about God. If we look at the human race we learn even more about Him. If we think about our *intellect, morality, conscience* and *emotions* we learn that God must be:

Good

  Righteous

    Rational

    Just

  Relational

Loving

When we throw all this information from creation together we learn that **God is** *the all-powerful creator and ruler of all things, He is good, righteous and just and we, as His creatures, owe Him our allegiance.*

 'What can be known about God is evident among them [humanity], because God has shown it to them. For his invisible attributes, that is, his eternal power and divine nature, have been clearly seen since the creation of the world, being understood through what he has made. As a result, people are without excuse' (Rom. 1:19-20).

If creation tells us that we were created by an all-powerful, good, and righteous God; if it tells us that we owe our allegiance to Him, then:

Why do we ignore Him, pretend He doesn't exist and live life on our own terms?

REENIE

Reenie is irritated by these questions, *'What do you mean we don't give a stuff about God? That's just not true! We believe in God. We're good people. Pete's worked all his life. I've brought my kids up well. I care for my grandkids! I go to church, I pray, I've even had my holy communion! This is all a bit heavy. Aren't you just taking this Bible stuff a bit too far!'*

STOP

What do you think?

GENERAL REVELATION

Bible teachers call this information from nature, *'general revelation.'* This information is freely available to every human being who has ever set foot on the planet earth. It's why we can say that **every person**, whether they're from a scheme in Scotland or a remote tribe in the middle of nowhere, **is guilty before God.**

Everybody knows He exists

Everybody knows we owe Him everything

Everybody knows we should obey Him

Everybody knows judgement will come

But nobody cares.

STOP

Having got this far and having understood these points, can you see now why the Bible exists? Explain your answer.

SPECIAL REVELATION

The Bible exists because *we are in grave danger* and *we need to be saved from the danger we are in*. The **Bible** is God's **kind**, **gracious**, **revelation of Himself** as the *lover and saviour of sinners through the person and work of Jesus Christ*. Teachers of the Bible call this, *'special revelation.'* Nature supplies us with enough information to know we are in danger, but if we are going to be saved, we need to know more than creation can teach us on its own.

 ## ILLUSTRATION

'Nan, can we go fishing up at the old black bothy this weekend?'

Definition: both·y
[both-ee, baw-thee] noun, (in Scotland) a small hut or cottage.

Before Reenie gets a chance to answer, Pete jumps in. *'Oh, do you remember that time we got lost going to the black bothy? We were on the old road on the way to Loch Fyne. Remember, it was late, it was dark, the weather was seriously grim and you lot were whining because of the cold. Even with the map we just couldn't find the place. In fact, it was pure luck that we stumbled on it in the end. I'd never been so happy to see the place, especially when the fire was roaring and the tea was made.'*

'But, grandad, that was ages ago, and we have been there loads now so we know the way. We've got google maps on our phones anyway.'

Pete chuckled from the corner, *'Seriously? What good do you think your phones are going to do up there? You'll get into trouble if you just rely on your gadgets. How is your phone going to help you when the wind starts up, the rain is pouring down, you're lost and cold and there's no phone signal? You'll end up lost and alone in the dark.'*

In a sense, we are all like this. We live our lives alone in the dark, battered by forces beyond our control or understanding, with a vague idea of where we'd like to be but no understanding of how to find safety. All the while we have no clue whatsoever as to how much danger we are in.

That's a picture of the spiritual position of every human being in the world unless God tells us how to be saved.

 'Your word is a lamp for my feet and a light on my path' (Ps. 119:105).

The Bible is a light in the dark to lost people. The Bible exists because God is kind, gracious, loving and compassionate and **He wants the people He created to repent and be saved from sin and judgement.**

STOP

Do you think that God likes to see wicked people die?

 '"Do you think that I like to see wicked people die?" says the Sovereign Lord. "Of course not! I want them to turn from their wicked ways and live"' (Ezek. 18:23, NLT).

The Bible is God's gracious communication of salvation to sinners. A pastor in America called Kevin DeYoung writes this:

'God speaks, and He speaks not simply to be heard and not merely to pass along information. He speaks so that we can begin to know the unknowable and fathom the unfathomable. You may think you've seen it all, and you've heard it all, and you've experienced everything there is to experience. But you haven't seen or heard or imagined what the God of love has prepared for those who love Him. This is the good news of the cross. This is the good news for the forgiven and the redeemed. And this is the good news you won't find anywhere else but in the word of God.'

The Bible is God's Word to man.

It is His kind and gracious revelation of Himself

It contains the story of salvation

It reveals to us that **the only way we can be saved** is

> **by faith in Jesus Christ.**

STOP

The Bible is God's Word but who wrote it all down?

The Bible is actually a portable library. It's a collection of 66 books written over 1,500 years by over 40 different men, in 3 languages: Hebrew, a little bit of Aramaic, and Greek.

The 66 books are a mixed bag of styles and genres. There are history books, biographies, genealogies, laws and rules, sermons, letters, a hymnbook, proverbs, poems, prophecy and (the always entertaining) apocalyptic literature. Despite these differences of style, *all these books reveal the same God and tell the same gospel of Jesus Christ.*

The Bible begins with the tale of creation and our rebellion against God in Genesis chapters 1-3. It then charts the unfolding story of salvation in Jesus.

The Bible splits broadly into 2 parts:

The Old Testament, made up of 39 books, written by the prophets – men like Moses, Joshua, David, Daniel and Amos. These men had diverse backgrounds, different life experiences, each instructed by God to record His Word. Men who tell the story of the people of Israel, a people chosen by God in order to bless the world and bring about the salvation of His people.

The 2nd part of the Bible, the **New Testament,** is made up of 27 books written by an equally diverse group of people, the apostles (eye witnesses to the life of Jesus) and their close companions – men like Matthew, John, Luke, Peter and Paul. These men tell the story of the birth, life, ministry, death and resurrection of Jesus of Nazareth, the saviour king, the fulfilment of God's promise to bless the world through Israel. These men record the story of the birth of the church, which is both the evidence and means of God blessing the world by saving His people.

In his 2nd letter the Apostle Peter tells us how these 66 books came to be:

'Above all, you know this: No prophecy of Scripture comes from the prophet's own interpretation, because no prophecy ever came by the will of man; instead, men spoke from God as they were carried along by the Holy Spirit' (2 Pet. 1:20-21).

In these verses, Peter tells us that the Bible is both the Word of God and the words of men. He tells us that it isn't a random collection of made-up nonsense, but that the men spoke and wrote what they heard from God as they were carried along and inspired by the Holy Spirit.

STOP

So, were these men who wrote the Bible just like God's robots? What do you think 'being carried along and inspired by the Holy Spirit' actually means?

 'All Scripture is inspired by God and is profitable for teaching, for rebuking, for correcting, for training in righteousness, so that the man of God may be complete, equipped for every good work' (2 Tim. 3:16-17).

These verses tell us that every word of the Bible, though penned by over 40 different men, is inspired by God. *Therefore, we know it can be trusted but it also means it must be obeyed.* We'll look at what is meant by inspiration in more detail in chapter 3.

Though the Bible has many authors and styles of writing it clearly reveals to us everything we need to know about God and everything we need to know to be saved from our sins and live godly lives.

Even though it contains many difficult concepts and challenging truths, its core message is:

God is the good creator and judge of the universe

    All human beings are sinners by nature and choice

        We have all rebelled against God

            We all deserve His righteous wrath poured out on us in hell

                forever

But, thankfully for us, it doesn't end there. It teaches us:

That God, in unimaginable love and kindness, sent His Son Jesus into the world

to live the life we have not lived,

   a perfect life that God requires,

      to die the death that we deserve

taking upon Himself the sin of His people and our punishment

      and that Jesus is raised to life so that we might live

   and salvation from sin and judgement come by repentance

and faith in Him.

This core message is clear; it unfolds on every page, and can be understood even by a child.

The Bible comes from a speaking God whose gracious desire is to reveal Himself and save ruined sinners.

It is His inspired Word, written by many men over 1,500 years in order to reveal to us everything we need to know about God and salvation from sin through faith in Jesus Christ.

 SUMMARY

The Bible is the very Word of God, written by over 40 authors that were inspired by God through the Holy Spirit to write His Word to us. It is able to make us wise for salvation, through faith in Jesus Christ, then make us useful to Jesus as we live out our lives.

MEMORY VERSE:

'The heavens declare the glory of God, and the expanse proclaims the work of his hands. Day after day they pour out speech; night after night they communicate knowledge' (Ps. 19:1-2).

WHAT'S THE POINT?
The Bible is GOD's completed Word.

2. WHERE DID THE BIBLE COME FROM?

PART II (CANON)

 PETE

Reenie was making the dinner as Pete sat at the kitchen table reading his paper,

'I need to give you your dinner early tonight darling. I'm going to go to the Bible study at the chapel.'

Pete looked up from his paper. *'You don't want to be paying too much attention to what that lot says. I was watching a documentary this week, a historical thing, about how the Bible was just made up of a bunch of myths and legends. Bits they pinched from different religions and the people from them days. They said it's like they took all the best bits and mushed it together to make up their own thing. I'm telling you, Reenie, it's all a bunch of baloney.'*

STOP

What do you think? Where do you think the Bible comes from?

It's little wonder Pete is confused. He watched a documentary where the host claimed that the 66 books of the Bible were put together by a secret council with a hidden agenda in the 4th century. In fact, according to this TV show, there are other books out there that tell a different story and that are being suppressed by the church.

The 66 books of the Bible are also known as the 'canon of Scripture'. That's canon, with one 'n' not two. This is a Greek word that means 'measuring stick.' A measuring stick was used to test if an object was up to standard. When we say something is canon now, it's merely a way of saying 'it's legit'.

STOP

You getting that? It's a weird word right but canon = legit. What makes something legit? What makes it trustworthy? Can you think of some reasons why the 66 books of the Bible are recognised as legit?

There are two common mistakes and misunderstandings when it comes to canon. The first one is to assume that somewhere around AD96, when the Apostle John writes the Book of Revelation on the Island of Patmos, the entire 66 books of the Bible fell out of the sky and were handed out to the church the following Sunday, in the same way as we stick Bibles on the seats in our churches.

The second mistake is to assume that up until the 4th century, some old dudes with beards simply decided to cut lots of books out of the canon just to suit their own agenda.

STOP

Why do you think it matters that we know how the Bible was put together?

 ILLUSTRATION

Reenie has a thing for jigsaws. She likes the 2500-piece ones and has a bit of a thing for kitten pictures. She buys loads of them and is always searching the charity shops to find cheap second-hand ones. To be honest, Pete's had enough and banned her from framing and hanging anymore of them in the house. '*There is only so much fluffy kittens one man can take!*'

Once, Reenie was feeling adventurous, and had three jigsaws on the go at once, a nice country scene, the London Eye, and a dolphin. She was working on all three at the dining room table when the boys got into one of their fights, banging into the table and sending everything flying. All the pieces were completely mixed up. Realising what they'd done, the boys helpfully scoop up all the bits into one massive pile in the centre of the table. Where does she start? How was she going to sort the pieces back into their own boxes? Pete, always ready with an opinion, said, '*I would try two things: Test if the edges fit together and check if the picture it makes is complete and makes sense. You've got to ask yourself: "Does it fit together?" and "Does it make one coherent picture?"*'

> **STOP**
>
> Think about the Bible, the canon. How can the jigsaw illustration help us think about how it should piece together?

As we think about recognising the true canon of Scripture it is helpful to remember that the same Holy Spirit who inspired the Scriptures is present and at work through the ages, granting the wisdom and discernment needed to separate truth from falsehood. We should also remember that God is the Lord of history and the sovereign ruler of all things.

 '*I am God, and there is no other; I am God, and no one is like me. I declare the end from the beginning, and from long ago what is not yet done, saying: my plan will take place, and I will do all my will*' (Isa. 46:9-10).

The task of recognising the canon was not accomplished by men alone. Instead, it was accomplished by God through His people.

So how exactly was this accomplished? We are going to look at this in two parts. Firstly, the **Old Testament** and, secondly, the **New Testament.**

OLD TESTAMENT CANON

STOP

Do you know what the first five books of the Bible are?

The first five books of the Bible are:

Genesis

Exodus

Leviticus

Numbers

Deuteronomy

They were written by a dude called Moses. Moses is the most significant and important human being in the Old Testament. His writings are the foundation of the Scriptures. These 5 Books of Moses, when grouped together, are known as the Torah, a Hebrew word which means Law. The Torah, or Law, was given to Moses directly by God on a mountain called Horeb in the Sinai wilderness after God had rescued His people, Israel, from slavery in the land of Egypt.

STOP

How wild is that! God Himself gave Moses the Law. What do you think was going through Moses' head at that moment?

These 5 books chart,

the history of the world from creation

through the fall

the beginnings of the story of redemption

the call of Abraham

the birth of the nation of Israel

their coming to Egypt

deliverance from slavery

the giving of the Law at Horeb

the construction of the tabernacle

the formation of the Levitical priesthood

and the journey to the Promised Land.

The Torah is made up of 613 commands given by God for His people. They are concerned with the promise of *life* and *blessing* for **obedience** and **covenant faithfulness** on the one hand. On the other, they talk of *judgement, curse* and *death* for **disobedience** and **covenant unfaithfulness**.

 'Keep my statutes and ordinances; a person will live if he does them. I am the Lord*'* (Lev. 18:5).

The Torah is really important because so many of the people who wrote the Bible, refer back to it time and again in their writings.

STOP

Let's stop and think it through because there is a lot going on here. Why do you think the Bible authors refer to the Torah so much?

This idea of reflecting back and referencing is known *as self-reflection* and this is one of the ways we recognise true Scripture.

Think back to Reenie's jigsaw illustration. Does it fit together, and does it produce one coherent picture? Likewise, the Scriptures connect to each other to make a complete picture.

'Above all, be strong and very courageous to observe carefully the whole instruction my servant Moses commanded you. Do not turn from it to the right or the left, so that you will have success wherever you go. This book of instruction must not depart from your mouth; you are to meditate on it day and night so that you may carefully observe everything written in it. For then you will prosper and succeed in whatever you do' (Josh. 1:7-9).

This pattern continues as the Old Testament unfolds. It builds upon the foundation of the Torah, reflecting back upon it and shows us the promises unfolding from it. As the prophets arrive on the scene we find them preaching the Law, calling the disobedient nation to repent and return to the Lord, by obeying His commands.

The consequences for rejecting the Law were clear:

'As the tongue of fire devours the stubble, and as dry grass sinks down in the flame, so their root will be as rottenness, and their blossom go up like dust; for they have rejected the law of the LORD of hosts and have despised the word of the Holy One of Israel' (Isa. 5:24, ESV).

The poetic and wisdom books, like the Psalms and Proverbs, also reflect and build upon the Torah as the authors consider what it looks like to live in obedience to God's Word or ponder the consequences of sin.

Here are two examples:

'The law of the LORD is perfect, reviving the soul; the testimony of the LORD is sure, making wise the simple' (Ps. 19:7, ESV).

'Those who reject the law praise the wicked, but those who keep the law pit themselves against them' (Prov. 28:4).

NEW TESTAMENT CANON

As we move into the New Testament, we find the Old Testament again being referred to and reflected upon. In fact, the New Testament begins with the family tree of Jesus and charts it back through the centuries and story of the Old Testament. So, for example, we read in Matthew 12:17, 'This was to fulfil what was spoken through the prophet Isaiah' (NIV).

'Today as you listen, this Scripture has been fulfilled' (Luke 4:21).

After His death and resurrection, Jesus meets with His disciples, and as He leads what was likely the best Bible study in history, He refers to the completed Old Testament.

'He told them, "These are my words that I spoke to you while I was still with you that everything written about me in the Law of Moses, the Prophets, and the Psalms must be fulfilled." Then he opened their minds to understand the Scriptures' (Luke 24:44-45).

This phrase, 'Law of Moses, the Prophets, and the Psalms' refers to the 3 parts that make up the Hebrew Bible of our Old Testament. Again, this pattern of reflecting upon and referencing the Old Testament is continued throughout the whole of the New

Testament as the apostles explain how Jesus is the Messiah and seek to instruct the church in wise living.

So, what about the New Testament? How did that come about? Who or what decided which books should be in the New Testament and which books shouldn't? Again, as with the Old Testament, *self-reflection* is key to understanding the process.

In the letter of 1 Corinthians (AD 53-54) we see Paul referencing the events of the Lord's Supper as recorded in the Gospels. At the end of 2 Peter 3, the Apostle Peter discusses the writings of Paul, stating that even though his letters can be difficult to get our heads around, the church must not ignore them because they are Scripture.

The church developed 4 criteria for deciding whether a book was to be accepted as part of the canon of Scripture. Think of them as the four 'A's:

Ancient

Apostolic

Agreement

Acceptance

ANCIENT

Does the book come from the right time?

APOSTOLIC

Was it written by one of the apostles or a companion of the apostles?

AGREEMENT

Does the book teach doctrine that agrees with the rest of the Scriptures?

ACCEPTANCE

Is the book accepted as Scripture across the universal church?

Let's take a look at an example of some writing that wasn't accepted into the New Testament canon. In a book called **The Gospel of Thomas** we read, '*Jesus said: When you bring forth that in yourselves, that which you have will save you. If you do not have that in yourselves, that which you do not have in you will kill you.*'

Now compare that with teaching from two books that were accepted into the canon:

'*But what comes out of the mouth comes from the heart, and this defiles a person. For from the heart come evil thoughts, murders, adulteries, sexual immoralities, thefts, false testimonies, slander*' (Matt. 15:18-19).

'*The mind-set of the flesh is hostile to God because it does not submit to God's law. Indeed, it is unable to do so. Those who are in the flesh cannot please God*' (Rom. 8:7-8).

The so-called Gospel of Thomas teaches that we can save ourselves by looking inside, whereas the true Scriptures explain that we are utterly unable to save ourselves, as all that comes from within us is evil. Clearly, we can see why the Gospel of Thomas was not included in the canon. Oil and water don't mix. The pieces of the jigsaw don't fit together and so the picture doesn't make sense. The same is true with the so-called Gospel of Mary, or the Gospel of Judas and all the other spiritual writings that sprang up between the 2nd and the 4th century.

By AD 367 we find the first completed list of all 27 New Testament books. Then, in AD 397, at the Synod of Carthage, a meeting of important figures from across the church formally recognised all 66 books of our Bible, which is now considered closed and complete.

 ## SUMMARY

Don't believe what you read online. There is no great conspiracy and hidden agenda behind the canon of Scripture. The books that make up the Bible were recognised because they are legit. The ones that were rejected didn't make the cut because they either lied about their authors, the dates didn't match and, most importantly, they lied about Jesus. We can have 100% confidence that what we have in our hands today is God's revealed Word to the human race.

 ## MEMORY VERSE

'All Scripture is inspired by God and is profitable for teaching, for rebuking, for correcting, for training in righteousness, so that the man of God may be complete, equipped for every good work' (2 Tim. 3:16-17).

WHAT'S THE POINT?

Every word of the Bible is GOD's.

3. HOW DO WE KNOW WE CAN TRUST THE BIBLE?

PART I (INSPIRATION)

So far, we have examined where the Bible came from along with how and why we recognise the 66 books that make up the canon of Scripture. We've said that the Bible is God's inspired Word, made up of these books, written by over 40 men over 1,500 years in order to reveal to us everything we need to know about God and salvation from sin through faith in Jesus Christ.

But what exactly do we mean when we say the Scriptures are inspired and why does it matter?

> **STOP**
>
> What do you think it means when we say that Scripture is inspired?

 'All Scripture is inspired by God and is profitable for teaching, for rebuking, for correcting, for training in righteousness, so that the man of God may be complete, equipped for every good work' (2 Tim. 3:16-17).

I'm going to ask you to do something silly, but it will help us to get our head around what the Apostle Paul means when he says: *'All Scripture is inspired by God.'*

Put your hand about an inch in front of your mouth and speak normally. It doesn't matter what you say, it's the fact you are feeling your breath on your hand as you speak that matters. It doesn't matter what volume you speak at. Regardless of whether we whisper or yell it's all carried out of the mouth by the power of our breath. Now, try to speak without breathing out. It's impossible!

When Paul says the Bible is inspired he uses a Greek word:

Theopneustos

This word means, *God breathed*. Some versions of the English Bible translate this verse: '*All Scripture is breathed out by God.*' Paul wants us to understand that the Holy Spirit empowered every word that the biblical authors wrote, in the same way our own outward breath empowers our speech.

STOP

Why do you think it matters that Scripture is breathed out by God?

This is important to understand because when we hear the word '*inspired*' used today its exact meaning is usually pretty vague.

 ### ILLUSTRATION

Reenie is a massive fan of the '*Great British Bake Off*' and watches it every week. This week involved baking cakes for special events and one of the contestants made an amazing fairy princess cake. This creation stood three tiers high, each covered in a different coloured butter cream, sprinkled with gold leaf and glitter, with a stunning fairy made out of icing gracing the top tier. '*Oooh doesn't that look gorgeous, Daisy (her granddaughter) would love a cake like that for her birthday next week.*' Reenie hasn't made anything so adventurous before but, inspired by what she had seen on the TV, she started on her creation. Five hours later, as she looked around the kitchen, her creation looked less like a cake and more like a squashed glitter mountain with a winged gargoyle slapped on the top! She'd been inspired by the TV show but what she ended up with was a bit of a mess.

We use the word, 'inspired' so loosely in our world today. We talk of a piece of music being inspiring. We talk of an inspiring half-time talk by a football coach. We talk of a sick child inspiring someone to run the London Marathon. In all of these examples we could swap the word inspired with the word motivate and lose none of the meaning. That isn't the case with 2 Timothy 3:16. The Holy Spirit didn't motivate the authors of Scripture to write. *He breathed out the very word of God through them.*

'*No prophecy of Scripture comes from the prophet's own interpretation, because no prophecy ever came by the will of man; instead, men spoke from God as they were carried along by the Holy Spirit*' (2 Pet. 1:20-21).

> **STOP**
>
> We have thought about this before, but what do we think carried along by the Holy Spirit means?

In 2 Peter 1 the Apostle Peter explains the inspiration of Scripture by saying that no true Scripture is written by the author's will, instead men spoke for God as they were carried along by the Holy Spirit. Imagine a yacht sailing across a lake and you get an idea of what Peter is getting at. The Holy Spirit carried the biblical authors along as a breeze carries a yacht across a lake.

When Peter says Scripture doesn't come from the authors' own interpretation, he is saying they didn't get a vague message from God and guess at what it meant. The Bible isn't made up of the apostles' and prophets' best guesses at what God was giving them. No, *the Holy Spirit moved in and through them* in order to ensure that His Word ended up on the page.

> **STOP**
>
> Why do you think it's so important that we get that the Bible is God's actual Word and not made up by men?

THUS SAYS THE LORD

'*Thus says the* LORD' is seen clearly and constantly throughout the Old Testament. Also, the phrase, '*This is what the Lord says*' is repeated again and again, throughout the writings of the prophets.

'*Moses and Aaron went in and said to Pharaoh, "This is what the* LORD, *the God of Israel, says: Let my people go, so that they may hold a festival for me in the wilderness*"' (Exod. 5:1).

STOP

The Old Testament writers constantly repeat the phrase 'Thus says the LORD' in the Bible. Do you think they were trying to make a point? If so, what point were they trying to make?

 ILLUSTRATION

Reenie grabbed hold of her granddaughter's hand and said, '*NO! Don't touch – how many times do I have to tell you?*' Even before Pete looked over he knew what his granddaughter had done. She had a fascination for turning the cooker knobs and watching the flames shoot out. Reenie was terrified she'd burn her fingers. '*You never listen. I must have told you at least a hundred times not to play with this! Go and sit on the step right now, young lady, before I smack your backside.*'

Sometimes we can be told something so often that we stop hearing what is being said to us. The Old Testament writers repeat the phrase, '*thus says the* LORD' over 400 times. The fact that the writers of the Old Testament repeat this phrase tells us that is something really important for us to listen to. They used it so often for a really simple reason. They wanted their readers and listeners to understand *that they were delivering the very Word of God to them.* This is what God says and this is what God requires of us. *This is an urgent and persistent claim found throughout the Bible.*

The authors are desperate for us to grasp this fact. **GOD IS SPEAKING** and **WHEN GOD SPEAKS WE MUST LISTEN!** The Scriptures tell us that:

God is

>   *the all-powerful*

>>   *all-knowing*

>>>   *creator*

>>>>   *sustainer and*

>>>>>   *righteous judge.*

He is the King of the universe. When I say King, I don't mean a figurehead monarch like we have in modern Europe. I mean an absolute monarch whose *word is law, power is unfathomable*, and whose *rule is unchallengeable*. In the book of Daniel chapter 4, Nebuchadnezzar of Babylon, one of the most powerful kings in the history of the world, says this about God:

 'His dominion is an everlasting dominion, and his kingdom is from generation to generation. All the inhabitants of the earth are counted as nothing, and he does what he wants with the army of heaven and the inhabitants of the earth. There is no one who can block his hand or say to him, "What have you done?"' (Dan. 4:34-35).

If the most powerful king on the planet recognised his powerlessness before the King of the universe, then it would be wise for us to recognise the same fact and be humble enough to pay close attention to God's word.

STOP

Read the following three parts of Scripture. What do you think Jesus believes about the Bible?

'Don't think that I came to abolish the Law or the Prophets. I did not come to abolish but to fulfil. For truly I tell you, until heaven and earth pass away, not the smallest letter or one stroke of a letter will pass away from the law until all things are accomplished' (Matt. 5:17-18).

'If he called them gods to whom the word of God came, and Scripture cannot be broken, do you say of him whom the Father consecrated and sent into the world, "You are blaspheming", because I said, "I am the Son of God"?' (John 10:35-36, ESV).

'He told them, "These are my words that I spoke to you while I was still with you that everything written about me in the Law of Moses, the Prophets, and the Psalms must be fulfilled." Then he opened their minds to understand the Scriptures. He also said to them, "This is what is written: The Messiah would suffer and rise from the dead the third day, and repentance for forgiveness of sins would be proclaimed in his name to all the nations, beginning at Jerusalem"' (Luke 24:44-47).

These passages from the gospels of Matthew, John and Luke, give us a crystal-clear answer to what Jesus believed about the Scriptures. He believed that they were:

authoritative

powerful

truthful

He believed that *every single word matters*. He believed that the Scriptures are unbreakable and could never be laid aside and He believed that they are all about Him and that they declare the way of Salvation. Jesus used the Scriptures to teach His followers and expose His opponents. When Satan attacked and attempted to tempt Him to sin, Jesus responded using the word of God as a weapon.

John Piper writes this.

'He (Jesus) taught that everything in it (the Scriptures) must be fulfilled; that the Psalm writers spoke by the Holy Spirit; that Moses's words in Scripture were the very words of God; that not one part of the Scriptures can be broken; that faithfulness to the Scriptures will keep us from error; that it can defeat the most powerful adversaries; that it is a litmus test to show if our hearts are open to know Jesus; and that it is a virtual script being acted out in the triumph of Jesus through His sufferings, death and resurrection.' [1]

To put it plainly, Jesus was and is a massive fan of the Bible.

VERBAL PLENARY INSPIRATION – VPI

So, let's answer the first of our two questions in this chapter; what exactly do we mean when we say the Scriptures are inspired? We believe in what Bible teachers call **Verbal Plenary Inspiration,** which is a fancy way of saying, every single word of the Scriptures comes from God. As we've already discovered, the biblical authors wrote exactly and precisely what God desired and intended to be written without flaw or mistake. This was achieved by the power and work of the Holy Spirit.

The LORD spoke

He carried the authors along

He breathed out His Word.

---

1   John Piper, *A Peculiar Glory* (London: IVP, 2016), p. 113.

Now you might be thinking; how does this 'God breathed', 'carried along by the Spirit', 'Thus says the Lord', 'VPI' stuff, leave any room for the personality and style of the human authors? We've said the Bible is written by God and human beings but it's not really a human book if God used the human authors as typewriters, is it?

That's a fair objection, but if that were the case you'd be right that the Bible isn't really a human book. Thankfully, that's not how it happened. All of the 40-plus biblical authors wrote in their own styles, displaying their own quirks and personalities.

Some are precise and particular

   Others are poetic

Some are technical

   Others simple

The Apostle Paul's grammar gets messy when he gets excited, whereas Dr. Luke from Athens has excellent grammar. More importantly, the biblical authors were sharing their own stories as eyewitnesses or they were recording the stories of other eyewitnesses of God's works. Their poetry and prayers found in the Psalms are reflections upon the author's experiences of God and His Word. King Solomon shares the great wisdom God gave him in the books of Proverbs, Ecclesiastes and Song of Songs. Paul writes his letters to churches he planted and pastors he trained. Daniel and John shared the amazing visions God gave them. The biblical authors didn't just write the Scriptures, they lived them.

The Prophet Jeremiah points us to the answer, *'Look, I am the LORD, the God over every creature. Is anything too difficult for me?'* (Jer. 32:27).

There is nothing too difficult for God. He doesn't have to work the biblical authors like puppets in order to get His word on to the page. His sovereignty means He is able to order and shape the lives of the authors so that their education, experiences, lifestyle, family, friends and culture, combined with the inspiration of the Holy Spirit, led them to write His words exactly as He wanted them written.

 'I am God, and there is no other; I am God, and no one is like me. I declare the end from the beginning, and from long ago what is not yet done, saying: my plan will take place, and I will do all my will' (Isa. 46:9-10).

God rules and **reigns** over all things and, therefore, *all His plans take place and His will is always accomplished.* Men whose lives were shaped and ordered by His hand penned the Scriptures He inspired.

STOP

Why does it matter that Scripture is God's exact Word?

In John chapter 6, after some seriously tough teaching from Jesus, many of the people who had followed Jesus from the beginning of His public ministry turn their backs and walk away from Him. In response, Jesus asks the twelve disciples a question and Peter's answer strikes at the heart of why the doctrine of inspiration matters.

 'Jesus said to the Twelve, "You don't want to go away too, do you?" Simon Peter answered, "Lord, to whom will we go? You have the words of eternal life. We have come to believe and know that you are the Holy One of God"' (John 6:67-69).

> **STOP**
>
> *Honestly, how would you have answered Jesus' question? Are you prepared to follow Jesus even when things get tough and He says things we struggle to accept?*

Life is full of big questions that need answers.

Where do I come from?

Why am I here?

Why is the world the way it is?

Why do people suffer?

What is death?

Am I good or evil?

If we turn our phones off and step away from the distractions of our lives these questions will crash over us like waves hitting the shore. They can't be avoided but, even more importantly, they can't be answered by us. When the crowds walked away from Jesus, Peter and the disciples stayed because by God's grace they had come to know that only Jesus has the words of eternal life. That's why Peter says, '*Where else are we going to go? You are the one who has all the answers.*'

In chapter one we looked at what the Bible is and where it comes from. We said that the Bible comes from God's gracious desire to reveal Himself in order to save ruined sinners. This means that **we have to take it seriously** and *we must surround ourselves with brothers and sisters who also take it seriously*. We need to be close to other Christians who help us learn and apply the Bible to our own lives.

We must be members of churches that

believe the Bible

   love the Bible

      obey the Bible

         sing the Bible

      pray the Bible

   preach the Bible

If that's not a description of your church then leave and find a church that it does describe.

 ## SUMMARY

Every single word of the Scriptures comes from God. The biblical authors wrote exactly and precisely what God desired and intended to be written without flaw or mistake. This was achieved by the power and work of the Holy Spirit. The Bible is where we meet Jesus. It's where we find the answers to the big questions because it is ultimately written by the One who has all the answers. It's able to make us wise for salvation and that is why it matters.

STOP

How will this change the way we treat and read the Bible?

 ## MEMORY VERSE

'[Jesus] replied, "Blessed rather are those who hear the word of God and obey it"' (Luke 11:28, NIV).

WHAT'S THE POINT?

The Bible is absolutely trustworthy.

4. HOW DO WE KNOW WE CAN TRUST THE BIBLE?
PART II (INERRANCY)

STOP

If I asked, 'Can you really trust the Bible 100%?' then what would you say and why?

In this chapter we are going to answer the big question: *can I really trust the Bible?* In the previous chapter we looked at what it means for the Bible to be the inspired Word of God. In this chapter we are going to learn how God's authorship of the Scriptures means they are absolutely true and absolutely trustworthy. We call this *inerrancy*. This simply means **God's Word is without error**.

 ILLUSTRATION

'Hey Pete!' Reenie shouted. 'Have you read this on Facebook about the guy in the white van trying to kidnap children up at the park? Apparently, he's a big, scruffy guy. He's got to be a pedophile. There's a comment on here that says the same white van is at the end of our road right now. Should we go and see?' Pete looked up at her and said, *'Honest to goodness Reenie, you're so gullible. Why do you believe everything you read? He's probably some random bloke nipping into the shops. That description could be practically anyone.'* Reenie points to her phone and says, *'No, Pete, it's true. It says so here and loads of people have liked and commented.'* Pete rolls his eyes and responds, *'Just because it's posted on Facebook, love, doesn't make it true. Worry about it if we see it on the 6 o'clock news. Then at least it will be legit and verified.'*

THE ORIGINAL AUTOGRAPHS

When we say the Bible is without error it is important that we recognise that we are talking about the *original manuscripts or autographs*, as written by the hands of the prophets and apostles. These documents were written on papyrus scrolls which were very delicate and because of this they had to be reproduced over and over and over again throughout the centuries.

STOP

How do you think we can be sure the copies they made of the original manuscripts were totally accurate?

Let's think about how we can be sure they made accurate copies. The scribes and monks who did this were seriously meticulous and they checked, checked and rechecked their work using many safeguards in order to ensure that the copies they were making were 100% accurate. We have about 5,800 Greek manuscripts to study and compare. That might not sound a lot, but when compared with other ancient books it is utterly staggering.

For example, we have about 10 manuscripts of Julius Caesar's *Gallic Wars* written between 60 & 50BC. The oldest manuscript is from 900 years after the event. Despite this gap, no historian is doubting Julius Caesar

John Piper writes, '*No other ancient book comes close to the wealth of diverse preservation that we have for the New Testament. Not only is the number of manuscripts remarkable, but also the antiquity. The oldest fragment we have, for example, is a papyrus that comes from about AD 130…. One of the oldest manuscripts of the entire New Testament comes from AD 350.*'[1]

---

1   John Piper, *A Peculiar Glory* (London: IVP, 2016), p. 82.

Between 1946 and 1956 the Dead Sea Scrolls were found in caves in Qumran, Israel. They had been preserved in clay pots and these Old Testament manuscripts are by far the oldest manuscripts we have. Incredibly, when they were compared with more recent manuscripts, *no real differences were found.*

STOP

Just think about that for a while. The oldest manuscripts ever found contained no real differences from the words we have in the Bible today. What does that tell us about how accurate the Bible is?

The meticulous work of these monks and scribes throughout the centuries means we can be utterly confident in the accuracy of our Bibles. What we have in our Bibles is an accurate translation of the very Word of God, preserved and protected by His sovereign rule throughout history.

 ILLUSTRATION

What an absolute nightmare of a day. Everything that could go wrong was going wrong. When Reenie woke up that morning the water boiler wasn't working, so she didn't have any hot water for a shower. Then, on the way back from the shops, the handles snapped on her shopping bag and she smashed all the eggs. Then she waited so long at the bank, she ended up being late picking up the grandkids from school. Just when she thought the day couldn't get any worse, Reenie missed the bus home. It was going to be 20 minutes until the next one. She was worn out when she walked into the hospital ward to see her friend, Kate. Her friend looked at her and said, *'Reenie, it's good to see you but you didn't need to come. It's pouring with rain outside. You're soaked to the skin.'* Reenie smiled at her friend. *'Sweetie, I told you I'd come visit you today and you know that I'm like always as good as my word.'*

The Bible reminds us that God is always true to His Word too. So, we know for sure that our Bibles are accurate translations of the original autographs. Now, let's move on to the question of trustworthiness.

> **STOP**
>
> How do you judge trust? Think of the people in your life who you trust most. What is it about them that makes them trustworthy?

It's likely the people we are thinking of are, *consistent, straightforward, honest and reliable.* When Reenie thinks about someone trustworthy she thinks of her dad. If he says he'll do something, he does it. If he says he'll be somewhere she can bank on it. If she needs help she can bank on him.

The trustworthiness of someone's word is a reflection of their character. Reenie trusts her dad's word because he has demonstrated and proven his honesty again and again throughout her life.

> **STOP**
>
> If asked, what would people say about your character? Do you live up to your word?

 'God is not a man, that he might lie, or a son of man, that he might change his mind. Does he speak and not act, or promise and not fulfil?' (Num. 23:19).

Scripture as the Word of God, reflects the character of God. *God is truthful, faithful, righteous, reliable, all-knowing and all-powerful.* This is why **we can trust every word of the Bible.** This verse from the book of Numbers ties together the word and the character of God. It draws an absolute contrast between God and man to drive home the point that God is 100% trustworthy.

> **STOP**
>
> Imagine you promised to pick a friend up at the train station at 10am tomorrow morning. Can you absolutely guarantee you'll be there?

The answer is no. We may give our word, 100% intending to be there to pick them up. But, we could get stuck in traffic, get a puncture, or trip as we leave the house and break a leg. There is an endless list of things that could leave our pal standing disappointed outside the station. There are an infinite number of things beyond our control that could stop us from carrying out a promise. That never happens to God.

God is not a human

He's not like us

He is always honest

He can never be frustrated or hindered

 'So God has given both his promise and his oath. These two things are unchangeable because it is impossible for God to lie. Therefore, we who have fled to him for refuge can have great confidence as we hold to the hope that lies before us. This hope is a strong and trustworthy anchor for our souls. It leads us through the curtain into God's inner sanctuary' (Heb. 6:18-19, NLT).

When the writer of the book of Hebrews wants to comfort his readers that their salvation is sure, safe and secure, he reminds them that God has given an unchangeable oath and a promise. **It is impossible for God to lie.** Solomon says the same thing about Him in the book of Proverbs.

 'Every word of God proves true; he is a shield to those who take refuge in him' (Prov. 30:5, ESV).

This verse ties God's truthfulness and faithfulness to the security of our salvation. It does so by explaining that it is God's unchanging faithfulness that makes Him suitable to be a shield and a refuge for His people.

Imagine you are fleeing from a massive storm. The wind is howling and gusting and up ahead you see two buildings. One is made of twigs and the other is a concrete bunker. Which one are you going to take refuge in? A refuge is supposed to be a place of stability, strength and security. *If it's weak, unstable or insecure it can't be trusted to protect you.*

We come back to this important passage again:

'If he called them gods to whom the word of God came, and Scripture cannot be broken, do you say of him whom the Father consecrated and sent into the world, "You are blaspheming", because I said, "I am the Son of God"?' (John 10:35-36, ESV).

When engaging His unbelieving opponents, who want to attack His claim to be the Son of God, Jesus reminds them that Scripture cannot be broken. Because God is God, His Word comes to pass. His Word is utterly trustworthy because God always speaks the truth. His promises can be trusted because God cannot be frustrated, stopped or impeded. The Scriptures are inerrant because God doesn't make errors. Kevin DeYoung gives us the simplest argument for the inerrancy of Scripture. *'Scripture did not come from the will of man; it came from God. And if it is God's word then it must all be true, for in Him there can be no error or deceit.'*[2]

'Sanctify them by the truth; your word is truth' (John 17:17).

---

2   Kevin DeYoung, *Taking God At His Word* (Wheaton, IL: Crossway, 2016), p. 39.

As Jesus prays for His people before He goes to the cross, He asks the Father to sanctify (make holy) His people by the truth before going on to explain how this will be done through the word of truth. Jesus teaches us here that the truthfulness of the word is what makes it useful for sanctifying His people. **The Bible** is able to *shape and renew our minds* to *correct, rebuke, mould, confront, conform, comfort, strengthen and shape* us **because it is inerrant truth.** In Romans 12 Paul challenges the church:

'Do not be conformed to this age, but be transformed by the renewing of your mind, so that you may discern what is the good, pleasing, and perfect will of God' (Rom. 12:2).

Every Christian needs the truth of the Word of God to set us straight and reshape us when we sin and believe false things about God.

AUTHORITY

The Word of God doesn't just reflect the character of God, but it also declares the *absolute sovereignty, power* and *authority* of God.

'Do you not know? Have you not heard? Has it not been declared to you from the beginning? Have you not considered the foundations of the earth? God is enthroned above the circle of the earth; its inhabitants are like grasshoppers. He stretches out the heavens like thin cloth and spreads them out like a tent to live in. He reduces princes to nothing and makes judges of the earth like a wasteland. They are barely planted, barely sown, their stem hardly takes root in the ground when he blows on them and they wither, and a whirlwind carries them away like stubble. "To whom will you compare me, or who is my equal?" asks the Holy One. Look up and see! Who created these? He brings out the stars by number; he calls all of them by name. Because of his great power and strength, not one of them is missing' (Isa. 40:21-26).

The Bible is not just a book of helpful hints and suggestions that we can take or leave as we please. It's the self-revelation of the creator, sustainer, redeemer, judge and king of the universe. The Bible reveals the will and commands of the king. Question 3 of the Westminster Shorter Catechism asks:

Q: What do the Scriptures principally teach?

A: The Scriptures principally teach what man is to believe concerning God, and what duty God requires of man.[3]

The Bible teaches us what we must believe about God and what God requires of us in response. **It is the first, final and absolute authority for the believer and for the church.** What the Scriptures teach is truth and the standards it sets are Holy law. *The Scriptures are the full and final authority for the church in all matters of faith and practice.*

STOP

The big question really isn't, can we trust the Bible? The big question is, will we obey it?

 ### SUMMARY

The Bible is absolutely trustworthy and without error. It is the absolute, unbreakable, final authority about everything. The Bible is God's Word given to us in order to reveal to us everything we need to know about God and salvation from sin through faith in Jesus Christ. **Will we come to it humble and ready to learn from God or will we proudly raise ourselves above it and ignore its teachings, commands and warnings?**

---

3   Westminster Shorter Catechism, Question 3.

5. HOW DO WE READ THE BIBLE?

PART I (THE OLD TESTAMENT)

So far, we've learned what the Bible is, why it was written, how it was written, how it was put together and what that means in terms of its absolute truthfulness, trustworthiness and authority.

But, how should we actually read it?

> **STOP**
>
> Is the Bible like other books we read? How do we think the Bible should be read?

Often, the Bible uses weird language (to our ears) and talks about things in ways that appear strange to us at first glance. Once again we are going to approach this topic in two ways. Firstly, in this chapter, we are going to look at the Old Testament. Let's jump in.

IN THE BEGINNING...

The first 3 chapters of the Bible set the scene for the whole Bible story.

Genesis chapter 1 gives us the big picture, wide-angle overview of creation. We discover that **God creates** everything *by the power of His word in six days* and that *everything He creates is very good*. The pinnacle of creation occurs on the sixth day as God creates human beings, male and female, in His own image and likeness. He then gives our first parents dominion/authority over creation along with a job to make more people and make the Earth suitable for them to live in.

Genesis chapter 2 zooms in and gives us a closeup view of the creation of Adam and Eve. We also discover that the Lord provides a perfect home for them – *'The Garden of Eden.'* We also read of,

the giving of a law for continued life and blessing

and the consequences of rebellion against God's law.

'The LORD God commanded the man, "You are free to eat from any tree of the garden, but you must not eat from the tree of the knowledge of good and evil, for on the day you eat from it, you will certainly die"' (Gen. 2:16-17).

Genesis chapter 2 ends with the marriage of Adam and Eve as we see God's plan for sexual relationships established.

One man

One woman

committed *to a monogamous*

life-long

God-designed

God-ordained *union.*

The final verse of the chapter almost acts as a cliffhanger.

'Both the man and his wife were naked, yet felt no shame' (Gen. 2:25).

Genesis chapter 3 is where it all goes wrong. The rest of the Bible deals with God undoing the damage of the catastrophic events that occur in this chapter.

In Genesis 3 we are introduced to *the serpent*. This cunning creature jumps out at us because, here in God's very good world, *we have a creature living in rebellion against God*. His only intent is to tempt and incite others to join his rebellion. Details about this serpent unfold throughout the Scriptures as we come to know him by many names:

Satan

The devil

The dragon

We read that the serpent tempts Adam and Eve to eat from the *tree of the knowledge of good and evil*. Tragically, despite God's goodness in giving them life, a perfect home, perfect companionship and a perfect relationship with Himself, our first parents believe the lies of the devil, eat the fruit, and rebel against God.

Disaster soon follows.

Sin and **death** *enter the world* as Adam and Eve fall into a state of depravity. Suddenly, the unashamed couple are hiding from God – afraid, ashamed and condemned.

> **STOP**
>
> Why do you think Adam & Eve are suddenly afraid of God?

We read that God comes to them in the Garden and calls to them. At this point we are introduced to a really important theme in the Scriptures:

God is not only the creator, sustainer and law-giving King

but

He is also the

holy and righteous judge of all that He has created.

God immediately dooms the serpent to destruction. The work of filling the Earth and making it fit for human life becomes painful and difficult, and *where spiritual death has occurred physical death will follow.*

'You will eat bread by the sweat of your brow until you return to the ground, since you were taken from it. For you are dust, and you will return to dust' (Gen. 3:19).

Finally, Adam and Eve are thrown out of the Garden of Eden. They are put out of God's place and presence and a Cherubim (scary angel name that means burning one) with a flaming sword blocks the way to the tree of life. So, what we find at the end of Genesis 3 is the holiness of God standing in the way of sinful man gaining life and entering into God's presence.

The great problems that all human beings share, are laid out before us by the end of the first 3 chapters of Genesis. *We see the reign and rule of sin and death and the inescapable reality of holiness and judgement.* These themes and problems will continue to unfold and escalate as the story unfolds. Our helplessness is exposed to us over and over again.

However, there is a ray of hope in the midst of God's holy judgement.

'So the Lord God said to the serpent: Because you have done this, you are cursed more than any livestock and more than any wild animal. You will move on your belly and eat dust all the days of your life. I will put hostility between you and the woman, and between your offspring and her offspring. He will strike your head, and you will strike his heel' (Gen. 3:14-15).

As the Lord promises the destruction of the serpent, **hope** is found. God promises that one of the woman's descendants will die to destroy the serpent. *'He will strike your head, and you will strike his heel.'*

> **STOP**
>
> Who do you think this woman's descendent might be?

Bible teachers recognise that what God is telling is, *'The first good news'*.

> **STOP**
>
> Why do you think it is good news?

Here, in the *middle of the disaster of the fall* and *the awful reality of sin and judgement*, comes **the gospel promise** that *one day the son of a woman will die to destroy the devil and his works*. He would bear the curse of our sin and die, so that we can be freed from death.

Chapter 3 has one more important thing to teach us. Remember the cliffhanger verse at the end of **Genesis 2:25**? *'Both the man and his wife were naked, yet felt no shame.'* Man's sin brought him into a state of *guilt* and *shame*. Recognising their nakedness, Adam and Eve attempt to hide from God.

 'The LORD God made clothing from skins for the man and his wife, and he clothed them' (Gen. 3:21).

God is giving a sign, that **a death is needed** to cover the shame of man.

This idea of death for sin is a really important theme in the Bible.

READING THEMATICALLY.

What is the purpose of our quick walk through of Genesis 1-3? The themes and issues we see here in these foundational passages of the Scriptures, *teach us how to read the Old Testament.*

The great problem of **sin**, **death** and **judgement** hangs over the whole of the Scriptures as an inescapable reality of human life. For every technological and cultural advancement made by humanity, we also witness *the advancement of sin and misery*, along with *the constant reality of death and judgement.* As we read the Old Testament, we will notice other themes, such as:

Messianic Prophecy

Kingdom

Covenant

Sacrificial Substitute

We are going to look briefly at each of these themes as we continue with this chapter. Understanding them, is one of the keys to really understanding the Old Testament.

MESSIANIC PROPHECY

The word *Messiah* means, **anointed** or **chosen one** and it refers to the promised deliverer/saviour. As the story of the Bible unfolds over time, we find a series of predictions concerning a coming saviour. *Understanding messianic prophecy will enable us to identify the Messiah when we eventually encounter Him.*

We have already mentioned the first of these predictions. **The Promise of the Serpent Crusher in Genesis 3:15.** *'I will put hostility between you and the woman, and between your offspring and her offspring. He will strike your head, and you will strike his heel.'*

This verse gives us a moment of hope in the middle of a complete disaster, as God promises that *the son of a woman will die* to destroy the devil and his works.

> **STOP**
>
> Who do we think the serpent crusher could be?

We meet Cain and Abel in Genesis 4 and we think, is the serpent crusher one of these men? The answer, unfortunately, is no. Abel ends up dead and Cain turns out to be a murderer.

Then we meet Noah in Genesis chapters 6 through 9 and we wonder if he could be the promised serpent crusher. It looks good at the beginning – he is saved from the flood – but, unfortunately, his story ends with him in a garden naked and ashamed. So, it's definitely not him.

In Genesis 12 we meet a massively important person in biblical history. We meet a man called Abraham. He is the *father of faith* and the *father of the nation of Israel*. God's promise of a saviour is expanded upon in Genesis 12 as the Lord promises that all the nations of the earth will be blessed through this man Abraham. We begin to think that maybe he is our promised serpent crusher. Yet, again, our hopes are dashed as we discover how flawed Abraham was. He often feared for his life and even passed his wife off as his sister in order to save his own skin. Abraham was a giant of faith, but flawed; he was not the promised Messiah.

In Exodus through to Deuteronomy we read of the rescue of the people of Israel (the descendants of Abraham) from slavery in Egypt. We read that they were given the law and of their journey to the Promised Land. *All this was happening under the leadership of Moses.* Is he the serpent crusher? No. In fact, shortly before his death, Moses speaks in **Deuteronomy 18:15-19** about God's promise to rescue His people one day:

"'The LORD your God will raise up for you a prophet like me from among you, from your fellow Israelites. You must listen to him....' The LORD said to me: "What they say is good. I will raise up for them a prophet like you from among their fellow Israelites, and I will put my words in his mouth. He will tell them everything I command him. I myself will call to account anyone who does not listen to my words that the prophet speaks in my name'" (ESV).

As the years go by, we learn that the saviour **will** be

a descendant of David.

He **will** be known as the

Son of God.

He **will** be

born of a virgin.

born in Bethlehem.

He **will** be

called a Nazarene.

He **will**

heal the sick.

heal the blind.

heal the deaf.

He **will** be

a Prophet.

a Priest.

a King.

He will be

hated without cause.

He will be

betrayed by a friend.

He will be

killed beside criminals.

He will

die as a sacrificial substitute.

He will be

buried.

He will be

resurrected.

He will

ascend to heaven.

He will

establish a new covenant.

He will

rule and reign

over

an eternal kingdom.

These promises build upon one another and create an ever-growing weight of expectation as we read through the Old Testament.

KINGDOM

The theme of the *God's kingdom* begins in the Garden of Eden. Here we see the shape and structure of the kingdom established.

It includes:

God's people in *Adam and Eve*.

God's place in *Eden*.

Living under *God's Rule*.

This theme, like the messianic prophecy, runs right throughout the Bible, from the *call of Abraham*, to *the promise to build a great nation* and the promise of *the land of Canaan*.

'*I will make you into a great nation, I will bless you, I will make your name great*' (Gen. 12:2).

The first five books of the Bible chart the birth of the nation of Israel. We read of their rescue from slavery in Egypt and their journey to the Promised Land. We read that God's presence with His people is displayed, firstly, in the *Tabernacle* (a movable tent where God agreed to meet with the people when they journeyed to the Promised Land) then, secondly, the *Temple* in Jerusalem.

As we read on, we meet Joshua. He firmly establishes the **kingdom pattern** of *God's people*, in *God's place* under *God's rule*. But, yet again, we discover that he is not the serpent crusher.

We are then introduced to King David in 1 & 2 Samuel as he becomes God's King. Could this be the one? Sadly, no. We just meet another deeply flawed man who chases women and kills to get his own way and hide his sins. However, we are told that this promised Messiah – who will crush the serpent – will come from King David's family line.

🔑 '*The* LORD *declares to you: The* LORD *himself will make a house for you. When your time comes and you rest with your fathers, I will raise up after you your descendant, who will come from your body, and I will establish his kingdom. He is the one who will build a house for my name, and I will establish the throne of his kingdom forever*' (2 Sam. 7:11-13).

The Kingdom soon falls apart after David's reign comes to an end. His son Solomon is on the throne as the people rebel against the Lord. The Books of *First and Second Kings* and *First and Second Chronicles*, along with the *writings of the prophets* chart the disintegration of the kingdom. They lay out God's judgement of His people as they are sent away from His presence and out of the land of Canaan, into exile.

Eventually, the people of Israel return to the Promised Land. This is recorded for us in the books of *Ezra, Nehemiah, Joel, Haggai, Obadiah* and *Malachi*. In these books we see **the walls of Jerusalem being rebuilt** and the **temple being reconstructed.** Yet, despite being back in the Land, there is no king and so the Old Testament ends with a grumbling people longing for a King and the former glory of the kingdom to be restored. The serpent crusher has still not come.

COVENANT

STOP

Covenant is a weird word. What do you think it means?

Covenants are *formal promises* or *contracts* between **God** and **His people.**

> **STOP**
>
> Can you think of a formal promise or a ceremonial contract that we might use today?

There are *two kinds of covenant.* Historically, there would be an ancient contract *between a king and his subjects.* This was known as a **sovereign treaty.** This covenant would begin with *a declaration* of **who the king is** and **what he has done.**

'*I am the LORD who brought you from Ur of the Chaldeans to give you this land to possess*' (Gen. 15:7).

'*I am the LORD your God, who brought you out of the land of Egypt, out of the place of slavery*' (Exod. 20:2).

The second type of covenant lays out *what the King requires of his subjects.* In this covenant there will be a list of blessings for obedience and a list of penalties for breaking the covenant.

'*The LORD God commanded the man, "You are free to eat from any tree of the garden, but you must not eat from the tree of the knowledge of good and evil, for on the day you eat from it, you will certainly die"*' (Gen. 2:16-17).

Leviticus 18:5 acts as summary of how the covenant works.

'*Keep my statutes and ordinances; a person will live if he does them. I am the LORD*' (Lev. 18:5).

The message is clear:

Obey and live,

Rebel and face the justice of the king.

The problem we read throughout the history of the world is that the human race is never able to keep to the rules of the covenant. We constantly fall into sin and disobedience. We are simply unwilling and unable to keep up our end of the deal.

> **STOP**
>
> What do you think the consequences are, for us, when we break God's covenant?

Let me repeat. **Sin** means we are both **unwilling** and **unable** to obey. If we are going to live under the blessing of the Lord, then another kind of covenant is going to be needed. A covenant that doesn't rely on the obedience of sinners.

> **STOP**
>
> Do we try to solve our sin problems by trying harder? What kind of ways have you tried to please God?

 REENIE

Nearly every second word Reenie speaks is a swear word. She doesn't even really notice how much she swears. It was just a part of her everyday conversation. But, when Reenie was around the people in the church, she was on her best behaviour. She worked hard to rein in her language and watch her Ps and Qs. But, as soon as she got home, the air turned blue.

There has been the odd occasion at church when a *'bad word'* just popped out. One day, when she was working in the kitchen at church, she burned herself and let rip. Another believer heard her and immediately challenged her from Ephesians 4. *'Don't let any unwholesome talk come out of your mouth.'* Reenie felt the anger rise up inside her. Who did this person think they were, throwing the Bible in her face? Reenie walked out, vowing never to return. But, try as she might, she couldn't get that verse out of her mind for the rest of the day. Lying awake that night she suddenly realised how bad her language really was. Almost every other word that came out of her mouth was an expletive. How had she not noticed that before? She began to feel heavy-hearted about the issue and asked God to help her control her tongue and clean up her language.

> **STOP**
>
> *Do you think that Reenie has truly recognised her sin is a heart problem? Why would you say that?*

 "'Look, the days are coming" – this is the LORD's declaration – "when I will make a new covenant…. I will put my teaching within them and write it on their hearts. I will be their God, and they will be my people. No longer will one teach his neighbour or his brother, saying, 'Know the LORD,' for they will all know me, from the least to the greatest of them" – this is the LORD's declaration. "For I will forgive their iniquity and never again remember their sin"' (Jer. 31:31-34).

 'I will give you a new heart and put a new spirit within you; I will remove your heart of stone and give you a heart of flesh' (Ezek. 36:26).

> **STOP**
>
> Obviously, the Bible isn't talking about a literal heart transplant. So, what do you think it means to have a new heart?

What differences do you see in your own life since God has given you a new heart?

 PETE

Reenie and Pete have been getting social security for a couple of years, ever since he got laid off from his work as a bus driver. Pete has diabetes and has suffered a massive heart attack. Not able to work and with no hope of another job, he eventually signed on for welfare benefits.

The first Christmas after he lost his job was hard. Money was tight, and Reenie took on a couple of cleaning jobs to help her pay for the grandkids' presents. Reenie and Pete didn't think to declare her income. In fact, they never even gave it a second thought. Everyone does it. Everybody does a bit of cash in hand under the counter. It doesn't hurt anyone.

It wasn't until a few months after they became Christians that it really struck them that what they were doing was dishonest. Pete was feeling guilty. He'd been talking to Reenie about going to the welfare to tell them the truth and admit they had been fiddling the system. *'But, why can't I just stop working?'* Reenie pleaded. *'We don't actually have to tell them, do we? I'm worried sick. What if we get in serious trouble or even get the jail – we just can't tell them!'*

STOP

Who is showing signs of real heart change? *Reenie or Pete?*

SACRIFICIAL SUBSTITUTE

From the moment that sin and shame enter into the world, **sacrificial substitution appears as a solution to the problem.** As Adam and Eve stand naked, condemned and ashamed, soon to be thrown out of the Garden of Eden and God's presence, God graciously covers their shame with the skins of an animal.

 'The LORD God made clothing from skins for the man and his wife, and he clothed them' (Gen. 3:21).

We learn a simple and profound lesson from God's gracious provision for Adam and Eve. For sin and shame to be covered, **a substitute must die, and blood must be spilled.** As the story of the Scriptures progress, this truth is brought into ever clearer focus. The story of the Passover and the rescue of Israel from Egypt followed by the establishment of the sacrificial system make it crystal clear that for sin to be covered a substitute must die. The Bible therefore directs us to Jesus who died to take away our sins on the cross.

 SUMMARY

The key to reading the Old Testament is following the major themes as they unfold over the years. Throughout its 39 books, different literature styles, and all its many characters, we can track the promises God makes along the way. In part one we have seen that the **Old Testament is a book of promises to come.**

In part 2 we will see that the New Testament is a book of the **fulfilment of God's promises**.

 MEMORY VERSE

'How can a young man keep his way pure? By keeping your word. I have sought you with all my heart; don't let me wander from your commands. I have treasured your word in my heart so that I may not sin against you' (Ps. 119:9-11).

WHAT'S THE POINT?

The New Testament shows us Jesus is the saviour.

6. HOW DO I READ THE BIBLE?

PART II (NEW TESTAMENT)

STOP

Do you remember what kind of promises we talked about in the Old Testament?

In the previous chapter we began by saying that the Old Testament is a book of promises. We highlighted a few of these promises and then looked at a few of the major themes present in the Old Testament.

In the New Testament we move from promise to fulfilment, as God makes good on His promises and brings His plans to fruition. We are going to pick the same four themes we looked at in the Old Testament chapter and have a brief look at how these themes find fulfilment in Jesus and His church and how the great problems of sin and death are overcome.

 ILLUSTRATION

Reenie always loved hearing stories from her nana about their family history. Her grandad had been in the Great War and got a few medals for bravery. When Reenie was a child she used to get all the pictures out and line them up along the kitchen table plotting the history of her family.

Last week she saw an advert that said, '*Who do you think you really are?*' It was for a computer program that helped create family trees. It was only £7.99 a month. *'Pete, I'd love to do that. Can you help me set up the account?'*

Everyone has a family tree.

Even Jesus.

The New Testament begins with this sentence:

 'An account of the genealogy of Jesus Christ, the Son of David, the Son of Abraham' (Matt. 1:1).

> **STOP**
>
> *Genealogy is a bit of a fancy word. What do you think it means?*

From its first words onward, *the goal of the New Testament* is to show its readers that

Jesus is the Messiah. He is the *'anointed/chosen one.'*

That He had come to

destroy the works of the enemy and

to save His people.

One of the main ways that the authors of the New Testament achieve their goal is to show how *Jesus consistently fulfils every prophecy found in the Old Testament* Scriptures surrounding the coming Messiah.

Matthew begins his gospel by giving us a detailed account of Jesus' family tree. A big list of names seems like a boring way to begin such an important book, but Matthew is desperate for his readers to understand that **Jesus of Nazareth is the real deal**. In the first chapter alone, he tells us that *Jesus fulfils three important prophecies.*

He was descended from David.

He was a descendant of Abraham.

He was born of a virgin by the power of the Holy Spirit.

All of this was just as the prophet Isaiah had promised more than 700 years before even Matthew puts pen to paper!

> **STOP**
>
> *How amazing is that? Just take a minute to think about it. 700 years before Matthew writes down Jesus' family tree, a prophet shared the details of His birth and heritage. What does that tell us about Jesus?*

There are *61 distinct Messianic prophecies in the Old Testament* and **Jesus of Nazareth fulfils every single one**. Now you might think this is no big deal. But you'd be very wrong. This is a massive deal!

 ILLUSTRATION

Reenie's man Pete likes an occasional trip to the bookies for a flutter on the horses. Sometimes, he will do the football as well. So, he knows how odds work.

Well, the odds of Jesus accidentally fulfilling *just 8 of the 61* prophecies are 10,000,000,000,000,000,000,000,000,000 to 1 against.[1]

Those are some steep odds, but they pale into insignificance when put next to the staggering odds for **61 out of 61**.

---

1   Peter W. Stoner, *Science Speaks* (Chicago: Moody Press, 1958), 97-110.

'One in a trillion, trillion, trillion, trillion, trillion, trillion, trillion, trillion, trillion, trillion, trillion, trillion, trillion.'[2]

Over the years many Jews had claimed to be the long-awaited Messiah and yet each and every one fell down at the 61 hurdles of Messianic prophecy. Until the coming of Jesus of Nazareth who is *the one* in a trillion, trillion, trillion, trillion, trillion, trillion, trillion, trillion, trillion, trillion, trillion, trillion, trillion. The Old Testament gives us signs, so we can recognize the Messiah when He comes. Many people before and after the birth of Jesus claimed to be the Messiah but not one of them has fulfilled those Old Testament prophecies. Jesus fulfilled every single one of them.

STOP

What do we think of Jesus now we know that He fulfilled all the Old Testament prophecies against massive odds?

The New Testament authors are desperate to hammer home the fact that Jesus fulfils every promise and prophecy of the Old Testament. They want us to **hear loud** and **clear** that,

The Messianic King has come and is coming again.

As we read through the gospels we should look out for all the times where we see something along the lines of: '*This took place to fulfil what the prophet had spoken…*'. In the previous chapter we noted that these promises build upon one another and create a huge weight of expectation and a deep sense of longing.

All of these expectations and longings are met **fully** and **finally** *in the person and work of Jesus of Nazareth.*

---

2   Lee Strobel, *The Case for Faith* (Grand Rapids, MI: Zondervan, 2000), 262.

The gospel writers saw Him fulfil these Scriptures. In **John 20:31,** the apostle says he wrote his gospel, 'so that you may believe that Jesus is the Christ, the Son of God, and that by believing you may have life in his name.'

HIS KINGDOM

The theme of God's Kingdom is expanded and fulfilled in the New Testament with the coming of the King Jesus Christ and the birth of His church. In the previous chapter we discussed the shape and the nature of Kingdom. It's

God's people in

God's place

under God's rule.

In the Old Testament, the people of Israel thought of the land of Israel when they thought of God's Kingdom. But, in the New Testament, we see that God's Kingdom spans the face of the earth and is made up of people from every **tongue and tribe and nation.**

So, as the New Testament begins with the announcement of the arrival of their long-awaited King, we soon realise that His arrival doesn't meet the expectations or desires of the religious rulers in Israel.

STOP

What were they expecting their Messiah to be like? Think back to what we discussed in the last chapter.

They were expecting their Messiah

To come in power.

To smash all their enemies.

To overthrow the Romans.

To reestablish the glory days of King David and Solomon.

But, it doesn't quite go like that! In fact, Jesus arrives on the scene calling the people to repentance and faith.

 'Repent, because the kingdom of heaven has come near' (Matt. 4:17).

Jesus announces that the Kingdom has come. But, instead of smashing the wicked Romans, **He calls the people of Israel to repent and trust Him for salvation.** He doesn't pursue the *rich, powerful* and *influential people.*

Instead, He lovingly pursues the poor, the oppressed, the downtrodden, outcasts, conmen and sinners.

His best friends are a ragged collection of working-class men and women. They are thieves, loudmouths and even a terrorist! He talks the Kingdom of God but **the Kingdom He talks about is totally foreign to the Jewish leaders!** In Jesus' Kingdom,

Those who are first in this life will be last.

Those who are last in this life will be first.

The proud in this life will be brought low.

The humble will be exalted.

The way to greatness is service.

The road to life is death to self.

King Jesus comes **not** *to rule and reign in the way the Jews were expecting but to serve and die* for His people. Jesus is,

The perfect servant rather than the mighty warrior.

A humble saviour not a conqueror.

 'For the Son of Man has come to seek and to save the lost' (Luke 19:10).

The salvation of His people is achieved through

His perfect life,

His sacrificial death,

His Triumphant resurrection.

(We'll look at these in more detail in the final theme of the chapter.)

After His death and resurrection, **Jesus sends His followers** out into the world to *preach the gospel, make disciples* and *declare His coming Kingdom* to the nations.

They are to go safe and secure in the knowledge that **King Jesus will return**

To *fully* establish His Kingdom,

destroy His enemies and

live with His people forever

in the new heavens and the new earth.

> **STOP**
>
> Now that you're a Christian and one of His followers what do you think that means for your life? How will it change how you live your life now?

 'When they saw him, they worshiped, but some doubted. Jesus came near and said to them, "All authority has been given to me in

heaven and on earth. Go, therefore, and make disciples of all nations, baptizing them in the name of the Father and of the Son and of the Holy Spirit, teaching them to observe everything I have commanded you. And remember, I am with you always, to the end of the age"' (Matt. 28:17-20).

The book of Acts tells the story of the **apostles**. These were men, empowered by the Holy Spirit, who took the good news of Jesus to the world. As a result, many churches were started. *These local churches were seen as embassies of God's Kingdom.* In these churches, Christians – *those who had repented of sin and trusted Jesus for salvation* – live in community with one another.

All the letters of the New Testament are written to churches and pastors by the apostles,

to help them obey the teaching of Jesus and

live holy lives in this world.

 REENIE

Reenie was at the shops on Wednesday night when she bumped into Audrey. Reenie and Audrey had been enemies for years. It went back to the time their children fought at school and, since then, every time they'd met there had been a slanging match. Once, it had ended in violence and the police had been called. Reenie hated the woman and that was all there was to it.

Yet, recently Reenie has been feeling convicted about her attitude towards the woman. She's been wrestling with the thought of forgiving Audrey. Then she heard a sermon on being an ambassador on earth for King Jesus, which really played on her mind. She was supposed to be more like Jesus and less like her non-Christian friends. So, instead of shouting at Audrey in the shop, she just ignored her instead. She felt so proud of herself for being like Jesus and being a good ambassador!

> **STOP**
>
> Every Embassy in the world has ambassadors, that represent their country. Do you think Reenie is being a good ambassador for Jesus here? What do you think Reenie should do the next time she meets Audrey?

Every local church should function as a witness to the watching world. *Churches exist to call all people everywhere*

> **to repent of sin and**
>
> > **trust Jesus and**
> >
> > > **come under His rule.**

Every local church also exists to warn the world that

> **the Kingdom of God is coming and**
>
> **that the King is coming back.**

Also, to declare that

> **there are some who belong to this Kingdom and please Him and**
>
> **others who don't and are under His wrath.**

> **STOP**
>
> *When people look at your life what does it say about who Jesus is?*

When King Jesus returns, **those who have not**

turned to Him in repentance and faith

will be cast into hell forever

where they will receive the just punishment for their rebellion and sin.

However, those who have put their faith in Jesus will be *made like Him* and *live with Him* in His eternal Kingdom. The Bible ends with a glorious vision of this event.

 'Then I heard a loud voice from the throne: Look, God's dwelling is with humanity, and he will live with them. They will be his peoples, and God himself will be with them and will be their God. He will wipe away every tear from their eyes. Death will be no more; grief, crying, and pain will be no more, because the previous things have passed away' (Rev. 21:3-4).

What a promise for us! What great comfort and great hope we have here for the life to come!

THE NEW COVENANT AND SUBSTITUTION

In the previous chapter we said Leviticus 18:5 acts as summary of how the old covenant works. *'Keep my statutes and ordinances; a person will live if he does them. I am the LORD.'*

Under the old covenant the rules were simple: *obey* and *live*, or *rebel* and *face the justice of the King*. However, the reality of sin means that people were constantly unable and unwilling to keep their side of the deal.

Therefore, another kind of covenant was needed. One that doesn't rely on the obedience of sinners. *This is exactly what we find in the New Testament.* It's here that we find **King Jesus fulfilling all the demands of the old covenant**, while **establishing a new one for us.**

STOP

How obedient are you in life? Do you always do what you're told? Do you always follow the letter of the law?

God is clear. The Law must be fulfilled. It can't simply be set aside.

We can never fully obey it.

Only Jesus can.

Jesus lives the *perfect life of obedience* **God requires** and earns the reward of life.

He takes upon Himself

> the curse of the Law,
>
>> the punishment for sin and rebellion
>>
>>> as He goes to the Cross.

In fact,

Jesus takes upon Himself the sin of His people and

faces the just punishment that they deserve.

Jesus is crushed under the full fury of God's wrath. On the cross He dies the death His people deserve.

Jesus met all the requirements of the old covenant for us, *obey* and *live*, *rebel* and *face the justice of the King.*

He took the place of rebels and so faced the justice of the King. All the time He was obedient to God and so now He lives.

The Resurrection of Jesus is the great proof that His life and death were acceptable to the Father and that He has fulfilled all of the Law.

Having fulfilled the Old Covenant, Jesus establishes the New. This new covenant requires faith in Jesus. The good news is that all who trust in Him receive not only His righteousness, but the reward of eternal life. *The Holy Spirit now grants new life to those for whom Jesus died.* We receive a new heart that now hates sin and loves and trusts Jesus. *On top of this, we now happily live in obedience to God. We do so out of thankfulness for His grace to us in Christ.* We are then baptised into a local church where we celebrate communion with other Christians. Churches meet together remembering Jesus' work on their behalf, including His great sacrifice, until we meet Him in death or He comes again.

 ## SUMMARY

From its first words onward, the New Testament clearly shows that Jesus is the Messiah chosen to destroy the works of the enemy and to save His people from their sin. He consistently fulfils every prophecy found in the Old Testament Scriptures that talked of His coming. As promised, He is a blessing to the nations. He is freely offered to all for salvation. **Jesus is 100% the real deal!**

 ## MEMORY VERSE:

'For the wages of sin is death, but the gift of God is eternal life in Christ Jesus our Lord' (Rom. 6:23).

WHAT'S THE POINT?

The whole Bible is relevant today.

7. IS THE BIBLE STILL RELEVANT TODAY?

So far, we've established that the Bible is 100% trustworthy. But, so what? Why go to all the trouble of reading it? I mean, what can an old book written thousands of years ago really have to say to our 21st century lives?

PETE

'Reenie, I keep telling you that you're wasting your time. That Bible-bashing nonsense is old-fashioned and pointless. I don't know why you spend so much time reading it. Pointless waste of time if you ask me,' said Pete, looking up from his newspaper. *'Well I'm not asking you, am I?'* Reenie was sitting at the table with her Bible open. It felt like every time she opened it, Pete started an argument. Sometimes, she wondered if he was right.

Like Pete, many people say that the Bible is completely irrelevant. So, let's look at two reasons why they are wrong.

Firstly, people confuse *relevance* with *popularity*. The Bible has many things to say on subjects such as life and death, the nature of good and evil, gender roles, sexual purity, homosexuality and marriage and divorce. *The problem many have is that what the Bible has to say conflicts with what our modern culture believes.*

For that reason, people reject the Bible as bigoted, narrow-minded and stupid.

Secondly, many people in today's society think that newer is always better. Therefore, because the Bible is an ancient book, it is considered to be useless to the modern world.

Let's look at these issues in some more detail.

CONFUSING RELEVANCE AND POPULARITY

 ILLUSTRATION

Suppose I know for a fact that you have a fatal, yet easily curable disease. Should I keep this news to myself or should I tell you so that you can get treatment? Why would it be bad to keep the news to myself out of a fear of upsetting you?

Obviously, I should tell you the news, bad as it is. Will this news be welcomed with songs of joy and unwavering happiness? No. I imagine the news of this potentially fatal illness will be entirely unwelcome, uncomfortable, unpalatable, and unpopular. Yet, it will also be the single most relevant and important piece of information you could possibly receive. What if your house was on fire but it's the middle of the night and you hate being woken up abruptly? Should I say, 'It's unfeeling and unkind to wake people suddenly in the middle of the night, I'll let them sleep!' No. That would be evil. I should call the fire brigade and attempt to save you.

The same is true with the Bible and what it teaches. It has some hard things to say to the human race. It tells us that the whole world is in **rebellion** against the King of the Universe. Because of that, the world is in grave danger of being **eternally crushed in hell**.

BUT

The King has made a way for us to escape this punishment. *By turning from our sins and putting our faith in Jesus alone we can escape God's punishment.*

Christians believe that the whole world needs to hear this message. Even though our culture thinks that what the Bible teaches is bigoted, narrow-minded and out of date, we refuse to keep it to ourselves.

Why?

Because we don't want people to spend eternity in hell.

 ILLUSTRATION

The world famous magician, and well known atheist, Penn Jillette (one half of Penn and Teller), asks a great question. *'How much do you have to hate somebody to not evangelise? How much do you have to hate someone to believe everlasting life is possible and not tell them that?'*[1]

Jillette gets the point we are making. *If the Bible is true* (and it is) then it's the most **important** and **relevant** news *in the world, whether it is popular or not.*

STOP

Do we know people who think the Bible is irrelevant to the world? What would you say to them now?

The main message of the Bible is timeless.

The truths of sin, righteousness and judgement to come, have never been popular. Human beings have never welcomed the message that they are guilty sinners. But they need to hear the truth, whether it is popular or not. Not to tell them, would be an act of hate.

---

1   https://www.thegospelcoalition.org/blogs/justin-taylor/how-much-do-you-have-to-hate-somebody-to-not-proselytize/ 18/12/2018.

THE BIG ISSUES

The Bible doesn't just bring us unpopular, but ever relevant, truth. It also speaks clearly on many of the big questions of life. It contains God's answers to questions we would otherwise have no answers for.

STOP

Why am I here? What is the point of life?

This is in many ways the most important question in the world. If we turn off our TVs, computers and phones, sit in silence and think about the world we live in, then eventually we will ask ourselves, 'Why?' The chances are we'll struggle for a meaningful answer. Secular science and philosophy tell us that there is no meaning and no point to life. They say we come from nothing and are going to nothing. We are told we're the result of a cosmic explosion. We are told that life is just a cruel joke, an accident and that death is the end.

But deep down **we know** that life is

> *too precious to be pointless,*

we know the universe is

> *too complicated to be accidental,*

we know the world is

> *too beautiful to be purposeless.*

We only find meaningful answers to our deepest questions inside the pages of the Bible.

The Bible begins with the simple fact that,

 'In the beginning God created the heavens and the earth' (Gen. 1:1).

This sentence means that the universe and everything in it, including us, *exists for a reason.* That means that *we have value and a purpose*, we are here for a reason. Isaiah 43:7 gives us that reason: *'Everyone who bears my name and is created for my glory. I have formed them; indeed, I have made them.'* **We are created for the glory of God**. That is a weird phrase but, basically, it means that we are created to reflect

the awesomeness,

> *holiness,*

>> *righteousness,*

>>> *beauty,*

>>>> *love and*

>>>>> *wonder of our creator.*

STOP

If this is all true then why is there so much suffering in the world?

Nothing causes us to ask 'Why?' quite like pain and suffering. Some people will ask how a good God can allow suffering to happen. *They think that the presence of suffering must mean the absence of God.* C. S. Lewis (author and brilliant dead guy) says this: *'We can ignore even pleasure. But pain insists upon being attended to. God whispers to us in our pleasures, speaks in our conscience, but shouts in our pains: it is his megaphone to rouse a deaf world.'*[2]

When we see suffering we ask why, because we know in the depth of our souls that something is wrong. We instinctively know that life isn't supposed to be this way. When we see evil people getting away with evil deeds or hear about awful crimes on the news, we cry out for justice because we know deep down that evil should

---

2   C. S. Lewis, *The Problem of Pain*: London, Harper Collins, 2002, 91.

not go unpunished. We feel this way because **we have been created in the image of God.**

The Bible explains

> *why suffering exists*
>
> *that God's justice will one day be eternally served*
>
> *about the reality of eternal suffering*
>
> *how to escape God's judgement though the finished work of Jesus Christ.*

Suffering exists because of the sinful rebellion of humanity against our creator. We were created with dominion over the world, but our rebellion brought death and decay into the world.

 'The creation was subjected to futility not willingly, but because of him who subjected it in the hope that the creation itself will also be set free from the bondage to decay into the glorious freedom of God's children' (Rom. 8:20-21).

This verse explains that even though the world is broken, and isn't as it should be, a day is coming when it will be made new and set free from the power of decay and the reality of death.

When **Jesus returns** He will *perfect those who trust in Him* and *He will perfect this world* and **we will get to live with Him forever** in a world of *joy* and *bliss.*

That final day will also mark the **end of all evil** and **injustice** shall be no more. Everything that we think has been swept under the rug will be dragged into the light and the King of the Universe will act as the righteous judge and His justice shall be done for eternity. In the book of Revelation, the Apostle John gives us a glimpse of that final day as he writes:

'Then I saw a great white throne and one seated on it. Earth and heaven fled from his presence, and no place was found for them. I also saw the dead, the great and the small, standing before the throne, and books were opened. Another book was opened, which is the book of life, and the dead were judged according to their works by what was written in the books. Then the sea gave up the dead that were in it, and death and Hades gave up the dead that were in them; each one was judged according to their works. Death and Hades were thrown into the lake of fire. This is the second death, the lake of fire. And anyone whose name was not found written in the book of life was thrown into the lake of fire' (Rev. 20:11-15).

Revelation 13:8 tells us more about the book of life. It describes it as, 'the book of life of the lamb that was slain' (ESV). That is to say that anyone who trusts in Jesus and follows Him will be saved.

Evil has an expiration date. **One day Jesus will return** and on that day all **evil will come to an end** and *those who love evil and reject Jesus will be thrown into hell* for eternity. There is nothing in our world more relevant than this news!

SUMMARY

The Bible is the most relevant book in the world. Only in the Bible will we find the answers to the deep questions of our lives. However, the Bible will challenge our beliefs and our morals, but don't confuse that with being out of date and irrelevant. His truth remains the truth throughout all generations, whether it is popular or not.

MEMORY VERSE

'God's divine power has given us everything required for life and godliness through the knowledge of him who called us by his own glory and goodness' (2 Pet. 1:3).

WHAT'S THE POINT?

Jesus is rightly exalted and we must trust in Him for Salvation.

8. HOW DOES THE BIBLE POINT TO JESUS?

The entire Bible is about Jesus.

STOP

Reenie asks, 'How does that work? Jesus doesn't appear until the New Testament.'

What do you think? Do you agree with Reenie?

Let's take a look at Hebrews 1:1-3.

 'Long ago God spoke to the fathers by the prophets at different times and in different ways. In these last days, he has spoken to us by his Son. God has appointed him heir of all things and made the universe through him. The Son is the radiance of God's glory and the exact expression of his nature, sustaining all things by his powerful word. After making purification for sins, he sat down at the right hand of the Majesty on high' (Heb. 1:1-3).

These verses from Hebrews begin by splitting history into two parts: **long ago** and **these last days**. An easy way to track the two time periods is by the two parts of the Bible, these are the,

Old and New Testaments

The writer of Hebrews begins by reminding his readers that God has been graciously communicating and revealing Himself to His people for thousands of years. The phrase, *'at many times in many ways'* is talking about *the different books and authors of the Old Testament.*

The phrase, *'the last days'* are marked by the coming of God's Son Jesus. These verses from chapter one in the book of Hebrews tell us that *Jesus is the great theme of the whole Bible* and that *He is the heir of all things.* Let's spend the rest of the chapter thinking about this.

Jesus is the Heir of all things.

STOP

What do you think the word 'heir' means?

The phrase, *'heir of all things'* means that

Jesus is the one who owns everything in the end.

He's the one who will inherit everything at the end of time.

That includes each of us.

 REENIE

Reenie says, *'Wait just a wee second now. Jesus owns me? No one owns me, not even Pete!'* What would you say to Reenie about this?

We must understand that **Jesus** is *the owner and heir of everything* and

everyone that exists,

will exist or

has existed.

But, there's more.

Jesus is the Full and Final Revelation of God

 'The Son is the radiance of God's glory and the exact expression of his nature' (Heb. 1:3).

This is a verse that can seem a bit strange at first. But, the author is telling us that *Jesus, the Son of God,* is **the perfect, full and final revelation of God**. *Jesus is the mirror image of God the Father.* That's what the author means by, *'the exact expression of his nature'.*

From the start of this book we have been saying that *the Bible exists because God desires to reveal Himself to us.* He desires us to know *what He is like* and *what He has done.* We noticed at the beginning of the book that He is a *speaking* God. He has spoken *most clearly* through His Son.

Jesus the **Son of God** is

the **Second person of the Godhead** (Trinity)

He **became** a **man**

in order

to show us **God** and

save us from our **sin.**

In John 1, the apostle John explains it like this:

 'No one has ever seen God. The one and only Son, who is himself God and is at the Father's side – he has revealed him' (John 1:18).

If we want to know what God is like, we need **to look at Jesus of Nazareth.**

STOP

Revelation may be a strange word to us. What do you think it means that Jesus is the full revelation of God?

The Scriptures are absolutely certain on this fact: *Jesus is the one and only saviour of sinners.* We can't reject God and think He is going to give us another way to be saved from His anger. We are either on Jesus' team or we are under His wrath. *There is no third way.* If we reject the Lord Jesus while we live here on earth, then He will reject us when we meet Him in death.

STOP

Where do you stand with regard to the gospel of Jesus? If you aren't trusting Jesus for the forgiveness of your sins, then what is your trust in?

The apostle Paul writes:

 'There is one God and one mediator between God and humanity, the man Christ Jesus, who gave himself as a ransom for all, a testimony at the proper time' (1 Tim. 2:5-6).

STOP

This is deadly serious. There is nothing more important in the world right now. If we do not stand with Jesus, then we are destined for hell. If you are a Christian, then take some time right now to pray for the souls of your family and friends.

In the Book of Revelation Jesus tells John this in Revelation 1:8, *'"I am the Alpha and the Omega," says the Lord God, "the one who is, who was, and who is to come, the Almighty."'*

But, there's more we need to know about Jesus.

JESUS IS THE CREATOR

 'God has appointed him heir of all things and made the universe through him' (Heb. 1:2).

Jesus is the creator of the universe. **Everything** that exists came into existence by His power. The Apostle John begins his account of the earthly ministry of Jesus with these words:

 'In the beginning was the Word, and the Word was with God, and the Word was God. He was with God in the beginning. All things were created through him, and apart from him not one thing was created that has been created' (John 1:1-3).

Jesus is

> *our designer*
>
> *creator and*
>
> *owner.*

 ## ILLUSTRATION

Pete was the kind of man that would pick junk from all sorts of places and fix it up. Bits and pieces of old engines and motorbike parts were always lying around the house. It made Reenie really angry at times. One night, Pete turned up dragging a broken-down old motor scooter with him. It was covered in rust and looked like it had been left outside for years. 'There's no way you're bringing that in the house, Pete!' Reenie shouted at him from the front door. 'Come on now, Reenie,' Pete said. 'It looks awful now but just you wait until I've fixed her all up!' Reenie wasn't convinced. 'Well, it stays outside. Another waste of money if you ask me.'

Pete worked on the scooter for a month and, slowly but surely, it began to look better and better. He put nearly every waking hour into making it roadworthy. It was his pride and joy.

One day one of Pete's grandsons came running round to the garden to see him. 'Grandad, grandad! Old Jack says that you didn't pay him enough money for the scooter and he says he's going to send some lads round to take it off you!' Pete was full of rage. The scooter was his. He'd rebuilt it from scrap. He'd patiently and lovingly restored every detail. He'd put his own blood, sweat and tears into the project. No way would he let anybody take it from him. He owned it fair and square.

We like to think of ourselves as *the masters of our own lives and destinies.* However, **the truth is**

> *We are not our own.*
>
> *We belong to the one who made us.*

The creator gets to set the rules for how their creation is used. If we ever wondered what all those commands in the Bible are, they are God's terms and conditions of use for the universe that He has created through His Son.

 The Apostle Paul writes this: *'For everything was created by him, in heaven and on earth, the visible and the invisible, whether thrones or dominions or rulers or authorities – all things have been created through him and for him'* (Col. 1:16).

This passage from Colossians tells us that *the universe* and *everything in it* wasn't just created by Jesus, **it was created for Jesus.** It is *His possession,* created to display *His glory.*

But, there is even more!

Jesus is the Sustainer.

 'The Son is the radiance of God's glory and the exact expression of his nature, sustaining all things by his powerful word' (Heb. 1:3).

Not only is Jesus the Son of God creator and owner of all things, *He also sustains all things by His powerful word.*

> ## STOP
> *Think about this carefully. We are breathing in and out and reading this book because Jesus is sustaining our existence. Our hearts beat because Jesus is telling them to. The sun is going down and coming up. The tide is going in and out. The earth is spinning and circling the sun. All of this is on the say so of Jesus.*

Jerry Bridges brings this point home beautifully:

'*Scripture teaches us that just as the Son of God was the agent of creation and is its present sustainer, so too is He also the agent of God's providence. Jesus is in sovereign control, not only of the physical laws of the universe, but of all the events and circumstances in the universe, including those that happen to each of us. If you have food today in your cupboard and refrigerator, that is as much the result of Jesus' care for you as was the feeding of the five thousand.*'[1]

This isn't a complicated truth, but sometimes it's hard to get our heads around it. **Jesus literally governs all things** that happen, **He is the sovereign King** of the universe. The simple fact is that *we can do absolutely nothing without Him*. He upholds the universe ruling all things for the glory of God and the good of His people.

 ## REENIE

> Reenie says 'I don't know that I can take any more. It's been so hard since Pete lost his job. We were just starting to get back up on our feet. I'm just so scared the social security decide that we have committed serious fraud and we end up getting taken to court. I know you keep reminding me that God is in control of everything, but it really doesn't feel like it. What if we end up going to jail?'

---

1   Jerry Bridges: https://www.ligonier.org/learn/articles/providence-jesus/ accessed December 17, 2018

STOP:

How would you remind Reenie that God is in control of all the details of her life? What will you say to her if she does end up going to court?

There's one more thing we need to know about Jesus.

JESUS IS OUR REDEEMER

 '*After making purification for sins, he sat down at the right hand of the Majesty on high*' (Heb. 1:3).

As we have so far learned, we are like Adam and Eve when it comes to obeying God. We choose **sin, self and rebellion** over **obedience to God** and the claims of ownership He makes in our lives. *The result of our sin is that we are under the righteous curse of a holy and just God.*

The wages of sin is death.

Because *sin is a crime committed against a God of infinite worth and beauty*, it is therefore deserving of an **eternal punishment in hell**.

But, there is **good news.**

God, in His infinite grace and goodness, has made a way for wicked sinners to avoid the just punishment we deserve.

He sent His one and only Son into the world,

He was born of a virgin fully human and

yet uninfected by our sin and fallenness.

Jesus did for us that which none of us could ever achieve.

He met the perfect standards that God required.

Jesus lived the life we have not lived,

for every second of every day.

He obeyed every command of the law perfectly.

 'The LORD God tells us: 'Keep my statutes and ordinances; a person will live if he does them. I am the Lord' (Lev. 18:5).

Jesus did this and then He does something else that is utterly staggering.

In the greatest expression of grace and love, Jesus goes to the cross. On that tree *Jesus dies the death that all who believe on Him deserve*. He was crushed under the fierce, holy anger of God. The prophet Isaiah wrote these words about the work that Jesus would perform:

 'We all went astray like sheep; we all have turned to our own way; and the LORD has punished him for the iniquity of us all' (Isa. 53:6).

But, death could not hold Him.

On the third day,

Jesus rose from the grave

    glorified and

        victorious over

            Satan, sin and death.

God kept His word that the righteous would live. Jesus was faithful to Him and therefore He lives! In addition, His resurrection is *the proof that He is everything He said He was* and that His work of redeeming His people was accepted by God the Father. He was raised to life so that we might live. *All who trust in Him for salvation* will one day **be with Him** and **be like Him.**

Hebrews 1:3 tells us that, *'After making purification for sins, he sat down at the right hand of the Majesty on high.'* Right now, **Jesus is sitting on the throne of heaven.** He is reigning over all things and one day:

> *He will return to gather His people into His perfect kingdom.*

> *He will judge those who continue in rebellion against Him.*

Until that day comes the King of the universe **commands all people everywhere** to **repent of sin** and to **put their faith in Him** for **eternal life** and **victory over sin** and **death.**

But, there's more. Not only did Jesus redeem His people from sin and death, He also redeemed the whole of creation. This is how the Apostle Paul describes it:

'For the creation eagerly waits with anticipation for God's sons to be revealed. For the creation was subjected to futility not willingly, but because of him who subjected it in the hope that the creation itself will also be set free from the bondage to decay into the glorious freedom of God's children' (Rom. 8:19-21).

Jesus allows for the universe to come under futility so that we would look to Him for salvation.

When Jesus returns *the universe shall be made perfect*, free from the bondage of decay.

SUMMARY

The whole Bible is about Jesus. Not only that, He wrote the story. He is God the Son, the second person of the Trinity and He created all things, sustains all things, redeemed all things and He is the heir of all things. **Jesus is the Forever King of the Forever Kingdom**. One day Jesus will split the sky open and *every eye will see Him*, and *every knee will bow to Him*. If we have trusted Him in our earthly lives, then we will be safe and secure in a future heavenly glory.

However, if we have chosen to ignore Him, deny Him and live in rebellion against Him, then we will be in deep, deep trouble. Revelation 14:10-11 tells us that all unbelievers, *'will be tormented with fire and sulfur in the sight of the holy angels and in the sight of the Lamb, and the smoke of their torment will go up forever and ever.'*

Today is the day, to trust in the only Word of God, King Jesus. Our eternal souls depend upon it.

 REENIE

Sitting in the doctor's surgery waiting for the doctor to call Reenie's name she was anxious. It wasn't overwhelming her like it usually would. She asked herself, 'Abnormal blood test, what does that actually mean?'

Before she was a Christian something like this would have consumed her. She would have been thinking and imagining the worst. To be honest, before she was a Christian she would have been afraid to come back to the doctor's at all. She had thought about telling Pete then about the test but, for some reason, she didn't. 'No point the two of us worrying', she had said to herself, but she had wondered if he would use this against God as yet another excuse to reject God.

It all seemed too overwhelming. She needed strength from somewhere. She reached for her Bible and turned to the daily devotion for the day. As she read it to herself she had the sense that the words were speaking just to her. Reminding her who God was, that He was in control, that God knows what He is doing – even in the hard times. She remembered pausing as she thought to herself, 'God's word is true and I can trust Him'. She didn't seem to have the right words to pray. She simply told God what was going on in her head. As her tears tumbled down her face she knew God was real, His word was absolutely true and whatever the Doctor said God would be there through it all.

She sat mulling over her memory verse '...*in all these things we are more than conquerors through him who loved us*' (Rom. 8:37).

Reenie looked up at the voice who called her name from the open door. She knew she wasn't in this alone...

 **9Marks**

This series of short workbooks, from the 9Marks series, are designed to help you think through some of life's big questions.

1. GOD: Is He Out There?

2. WAR: Why Did Life Just Get Harder?

3. VOICES: Who Am I Listening To?

4. BIBLE: Can We Trust It?

5. BELIEVE: What Should I Know?

6. CHARACTER: How Do I Change?

7. TRAINING: How Do I Live and Grow?

8. CHURCH: Do I Have To Go?

9. RELATIONSHIPS: How Do I Make Things Right?

10. SERVICE: How Do I Give Back?

IX 9Marks

Building Healthy Churches

9Marks exists to equip church leaders with a biblical vision and practical resources for displaying God's glory to the nations through healthy churches.

To that end, we want to see churches characterized by these nine marks of health:

1   Expositional Preaching
2   Biblical Theology
3   A Biblical Understanding of the Gospel
4   A Biblical Understanding of Conversion
5   A Biblical Understanding of Evangelism
6   Biblical Church Membership
7   Biblical Church Discipline
8   Biblical Discipleship
9   Biblical Church Leadership

Find more titles at

www.9Marks.org

20schemes
Gospel Churches for Scotland's Poorest

20schemes exists to bring gospel hope to Scotland's poorest communities through the revitalisation and planting of healthy, gospel-preaching churches, ultimately led by a future generation of indigenous church leaders.

> '*If we are really going to see a turnaround in the lives of residents in our poorest communities, then we have to embrace a radical and long-term strategy which will bring gospel-hope to untold thousands.*'
>
> **MEZ MCCONNELL,** Ministry Director

We believe that building healthy churches in Scotland's poorest communities will bring true, sustainable, and long-term renewal to countless lives.

THE NEED IS URGENT

Learn more about our work and how to partner with us at:

20SCHEMES.COM
TWITTER.COM/20SCHEMES
FACEBOOK.COM/20SCHEMES
INSTAGRAM.COM/20SCHEMES

Also available in the First Steps series…

GOD

IS HE OUT THERE?

MEZ MCCONNELL

978-1-5271-0296-5

GOD – IS HE OUT THERE?

MEZ MCCONNELL

So you're new to the whole Christianity thing. You've heard a bit about it but you aren't really sure what to do next and you've still got some pretty big questions. Well, the First Steps series is here to help.

Let's start out with the most important question of all: is God out there? How can we know if He exists? If He does exist, what is He like? What does any of it have to do with us? This short book will help you think through these and other crucial questions.

A bangin' little book for those asking life's big questions…especially those who don't know about Jesus!

Dai Hankey

Cheeky git and gospel ninja! (and Pastor of Hill City Church, Pontnewynydd)

… brilliantly simple and accessible to anyone searching for answers about God and truth, and yet biblically sound and clear about what it truly means to know Christ and walk with him. Mez has a sensitive pastor's heart and a burden for the urban poor that oozes with every page. This book is a clear and needed contribution from one of the most careful and wise thinkers on caring for the poor in our generation.

Brian Croft

Pastor, Auburndale Baptist Church
and Senior Fellow of the Mathena Center for Church Revitalization,
The Southern Baptist Theological Seminary, Louisville, Kentucky

IX **9Marks** | First Steps Of Discipleship Series

WAR

WHY DID LIFE JUST GET HARDER?

MEZ MCCONNELL

978-1-5271-0297-2

WAR – WHY DID LIFE JUST GET HARDER?

MEZ MCCONNELL

All too often, our heads can feel like they are caught in a dark, lonely battle between what we want to do and what we know we should do. God feels distant and we feel dirty. The second book in the First Steps series tackles the fundamental, day-to-day difficulties experienced by every Christian, and looks at the question, Why Did Life Just Get Harder?

If you want a book about the real and daily struggles of following Christ which pulls no punches, dodges no controversy, fudges no issue and gives it to you straight, then here it is.

Steve Timmis
Executive Director of the Acts 29 Network

Mez is one of us and he writes like one of us. This shows as he communicates biblical truths in a way that hits the heart and mind whilst giving a realistic picture of the joy and struggles faced by Christians.

Ian Williamson
Pastor, New Life Church, Middlesbrough

Too many believe that Jesus is supposed to take away all of their problems. This book will help me explain to them that the spiritual life is war. Mez keeps it real and speaks truth. I love this guy.

Joel Kurtz
Pastor, The Garden, Baltimore, Maryland

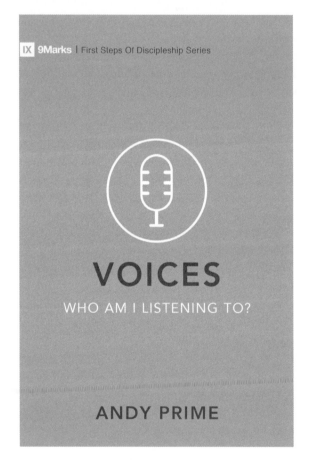

IX 9Marks | First Steps Of Discipleship Series

VOICES

WHO AM I LISTENING TO?

ANDY PRIME

978-1-5271-0298-9

VOICES – WHO AM I LISTENING TO?

ANDY PRIME

Life is so confusing! There are a myriad of voices clambering for our attention – which one is the 'right' one? Decisions, rather than being biblical, or good, or even moral, often feel like a stab in the dark, hoping for the best. This third title in the First Steps series looks at the wisdom offered in the book of Proverbs. God has not left us to navigate life as best we can alone – guidance is waiting if we only take the time to look.

Andy has shone a spotlight on the life-changing truths of the book of Proverbs, made sense of them in the overall bible story, connected them to Jesus at the centre, and then parked them right where you live.

Chris Green

Vicar, St. James Muswell Hill, London and Author of *Assemble the People Before Me: The Message of the Church*

Voices captures the inner dialogue in our heads and hearts that distract and deceive us, seeking to lure us away from Jesus. It winsomely offers life and freedom from Proverbs, helping us to see how God's wise voice is warning and inviting us to come to him, where true joy and everlasting love are experienced.

Robert K. Cheong

Pastor of Care and Counseling, Sojourn Community Church, Louisville, Kentucky and Author of *God Redeeming His Bride: A Handbook for Church Discipline*

Christian Focus Publications

Our mission statement –

STAYING FAITHFUL

In dependence upon God we seek to impact the world through literature faithful to His infallible Word, the Bible. Our aim is to ensure that the Lord Jesus Christ is presented as the only hope to obtain forgiveness of sin, live a useful life and look forward to heaven with Him.

Our books are published in four imprints:

CHRISTIAN
FOCUS

Popular works including biographies, commentaries, basic doctrine and Christian living.

CHRISTIAN
HERITAGE

Books representing some of the best material from the rich heritage of the church.

MENTOR

Books written at a level suitable for Bible College and seminary students, pastors, and other serious readers. The imprint includes commentaries, doctrinal studies, examination of current issues and church history.

CF4•K

Children's books for quality Bible teaching and for all age groups: Sunday school curriculum, puzzle and activity books; personal and family devotional titles, biographies and inspirational stories – because you are never too young to know Jesus!

Christian Focus Publications Ltd,
Geanies House, Fearn, Ross-shire,
IV20 1TW, Scotland, United Kingdom.
www.christianfocus.com
blog.christianfocus.com